A BLACK WOMAN'S GUIDE TO GETTING FREE

A BLACK WOMAN'S GUIDE TO GETTING FREE

TAMARA WINFREY HARRIS

BK

Berrett–Koehler Publishers, Inc.

Berrett-Koehler Publishers, Inc.
1333 Broadway, Suite 1000
Oakland, CA 94612-1921
Tel: (510) 817-2277
Fax: (510) 817-2278
www.bkconnection.com

ORDERING INFORMATION

Quantity sales. Special discounts are available on quantity purchases by corporations, associations, and others. For details, contact the "Special Sales Department" at the Berrett-Koehler address above.

Individual sales. Berrett-Koehler publications are available through most bookstores. They can also be ordered directly from Berrett-Koehler: Tel: (800) 929-2929; Fax: (802) 864-7626; www.bkconnection.com.

Orders for college textbook / course adoption use. Please contact Berrett-Koehler: Tel: (800) 929-2929; Fax: (802) 864-7626.

Distributed to the U.S. trade and internationally by Penguin Random House Publisher Services.

Berrett-Koehler and the BK logo are registered trademarks of Berrett-Koehler Publishers, Inc.

Printed in Canada

Berrett-Koehler books are printed on long-lasting acid-free paper. When it is available, we choose paper that has been manufactured by environmentally responsible processes. These may include using trees grown in sustainable forests, incorporating recycled paper, minimizing chlorine in bleaching, or recycling the energy produced at the paper mill.

Library of Congress Cataloging-in-Publication Data

Names: Winfrey Harris, Tamara, author.
Title: A Black woman's guide to getting free / Tamara Winfrey Harris.
Description: First edition. | Oakland, CA : Berrett-Koehler Publishers, Inc., [2024] |
    Includes bibliographical references and index.
Identifiers: LCCN 2023054059 (print) | LCCN 2023054060 (ebook) | ISBN 9781523006915
    (paperback) | ISBN 9781523006922 (pdf) | ISBN 9781523006939 (epub)
Subjects: LCSH: African American women—Psychology. | Self-realization in women. |
    Success—Psychological aspects. | Liberty—Psychological aspects.
Classification: LCC E185.86 .W55638 2024 (print) | LCC E185.86 (ebook) |
    DDC 155.2082--dc23/eng/20240228
LC record available at https://lccn.loc.gov/2023054059
LC ebook record available at https://lccn.loc.gov/2023054060

First Edition

31 30 29 28 27 26 25 24   10 9 8 7 6 5 4 3 2 1

Book producer and text designer: Happenstance Type-O-Rama
Cover designer: Naomi Silverio

For the healers:

Nikki Myers,

Dr. Sonya Broadnax,

and Jaymi Anderson

CONTENTS

PREFACE

Despite appearances, good things do happen on the platform formerly known as Twitter. I met Suzanne Walsh, the president of Bennett College, a historically Black women's institution, on the then–bird app and discovered a kindred spirit. She and I traded thoughts on how misogynoir can keep Black women ensnared and prevent us from thriving authentically. I told her about the pathway to Black femme freedom I was writing into existence for this book. And she invited me to share it with Bennett students, alumnae, and faculty. In the spring of 2022, I was the college's first-ever LiberateHer-in-Residence.

During one week on Bennett's campus in Greensboro, North Carolina, I led students and faculty on a Liberation Walk and discussed how the biased way society views Black women can trouble how we view ourselves. Students and I debated the costs and benefits of sexual freedom. Young women bore their pain as I helped them process how to manage relationships with sisters who are less than sisterly. I dropped in on sociology and women's studies classes to discuss how we might collectively free our minds from the burdens of sexism and racism. I led my first-ever in-person yoga class as a newly minted instructor; students and faculty joined me to greet the day with early morning movement. And one professor—a fellow yogi and sorority sister—treated me to a bottle of Cheerwine, a peculiar cola/cherry drink Greensborians love.

My week at Bennett College was an affirmation of my work. It is a unique honor to do Black femme liberation work in a place designed specifically for the education and growth of Black women—a space bursting with brilliant Black womanhood. It was inspiring. It was transformative. It gave me clarity. I felt whole. And from the warm response I received from Bennett Belles, I believe they felt the same.

But on my last day on campus, as I sat in the pulpit of the college's Anne Merner Pfeiffer Chapel, preparing to give a keynote speech for the college's Charter Day, I was not thinking about affirmation and collective transformation. I was thinking about my knees.

Let me explain.

I cannot hold my knees together—not in the way that women are told to be "ladylike." My thighs are fat. For most of my life, the rest of me has been fat, too. But even at my thinnest, my thighs have been thick. If I try to make my knees touch, the flesh between them resists and pushes back. Crossing my legs at the knee is out of the question. My fat thighs hide what is between my legs until I want it to be seen; I am not indecent. But my knees are always parted.

More than thirty years before I visited Bennett College, I sat on another stage. I was seventeen in June of 1987 and soon to embark on my own college journey. I joined 344 other Roosevelt High School seniors for a graduation ceremony at the Genesis Convention Center in Gary, Indiana. My academic performance had earned me a place on the dais with a handful of other students. I was third in my class, with a 4.02 GPA and the option of a full ride to three different universities. I was proud of myself. And I was proud that I had made my parents and grandparents proud. That is, until Mrs. So-and-so found my mother after the graduation ceremony and said to her, "You must be so embarrassed." This woman had noted that I sat on that stage, collecting my accolades, with my knees apart. Four years of academic excellence be damned; my inability to make my body conform to respectable feminine comportment was an embarrassment.

Respectability and acceptability in America are historically defined by adherence to White, middle-class, Judeo-Christian, heteronormative, patriarchal, capitalist habits and values—a reality that leaves a bunch of folks on the wrong side of right, including Black women like me. I am respectable in many of the ways our sexist and racist society demands of Black women. I was raised middle class by parents with advanced degrees. My parents have been married for more than fifty years, as their parents were. Like my parents, I am a member of several Black legacy organizations; I had an NAACP lifetime membership before I could walk. I can code-switch like a champion, but rarely need to use anything other than my natural flat Upper Midwest contralto. I am married to a man. My skin is a shade of brown people seem to be able to abide if they must abide Blackness. I am educated. I am a not-for-profit executive and a published author.

But when it comes to the ways stereotypes affect how Black women are seen, it is my body that has been my battleground.

I am a Black woman with a large body. I have been thick. I have been overweight. I have been fat. I have been obese.

In her book *Fearing the Black Body*, Sabrina Strings proves the link between anti-fatness and anti-Blackness, illuminating how fatness became a sign of immorality, societal rot, and menace associated with Blackness, and how Black women became the target for fear of fatness. As marauding European colonizers worked to prove their alleged superiority with spurious science, Black women were often singled out to stand as examples of physical deficiency and otherness. Strings quotes French anthropologist Julien-Joseph Virey, who wrote in his 1801 *Histoire naturelle du genre humain* ("Natural History of Man") about African-descended women's "big bottoms and bellies that push out" and how "the derrieres of Hottentot women resembled those of four-legged creatures, at times growing so large that they could be supported with a small cart, like a domesticated animal."

The American Mammy stereotype was woven using this fiber. The Mammy archetype cemented fat femme bodies (and dark skin, coarse hair, and broad features) as the hallmark of beasts of burdens—strong, sturdy, and built for servitude—and the opposite of lithe, light-skinned, long-haired, light-eyed feminine beauty. Still today, big, Black women are rarely seen as beautiful, respectable, or worthy by the White majority or by Black communities and other communities of color who have absorbed biased ideas of human worth.

It doesn't matter how lovely we are. Fat Black women are Madea, Big Momma, Rasputia*—the uncomely butt of the joke. Fat Black women are the tireless nurturers—big bosoms for other folks to bury their burdens in, workhorses. Fat Black women are the faces of socioeconomic disadvantage, "welfare queens"—even though the woman whose story Ronald Reagan used to construct that false label was neither fat nor Black.[1]

In some quarters, we may squeeze through a loophole to attractiveness by being fat in the right way—all big ass and titties, with a flat stomach. But this sort of fatness is about sexual attraction: Black women as sirens with ripe bodies made for male objectification. It calls to mind the sexually voracious Jezebel, a different box folks try to jam Black women into.

In "respectable" spaces, I am almost always keenly aware of my big body (and locs and tattooed forearms). I am aware of my willful knees that will not touch, even surrounded by love and support in the hallowed pulpit of Bennett College's chapel, a place designed for the uplift of Black women. Misogynoir is a sneaky thief that robs us at the most unexpected times.

With all the advantages I have, the biased narrative of Black womanhood can make me believe, even in a moment of triumph or achievement, that I need fixing. It can keep me from recognizing and choosing my authentic self, who is unconditionally valuable and worthy of love and regard. At times, it pulls me away from the conviction that my largeness and Blackness do not erase my beauty or intelligence or accomplishments or worthiness, or need for love and care. It keeps

---

* These references and others that may be new to you are defined in the glossary at the end of the book.

me studying my knees when I could be looking up at all the love and possibility that surrounds me.

In my first book, *The Sisters Are Alright: Changing the Broken Narrative of Black Women in America*, I explored not only how the centuries-old sexist and racist stereotypes—of the servile, asexual, burden-bearing Mammy; the strong, raging, and aggressive Sapphire; the hypersexual Jezebel; and the emasculating, indiscriminately breeding Matriarch—continue to influence how negatively Black women are viewed by society but also, and worse, how these broken narratives color our self-perception, making it difficult for us to move boldly and authentically and weakening our relationships with our sisters. I spoke to more than one hundred Black women for that book and have continued the dialogue in the seven years since its debut. I know, well, that I am not the only Black woman who sometimes finds herself living in reference to those caricatures—trying to outrun them, fix the things about myself they tell me are mistakes, and wedge myself into society's picture of acceptable and respectable Black womanhood.

For instance, a thirty-something sister from New York once told me, "I police myself on the way that I dress, the way that I joke.... I feel like I have to act really formal in spaces where others are not as guarded."[2]

If a sister cannot choose herself when she gets dressed in the morning, how will she choose herself when the stakes are higher? Every day, many Black women bend and twist to be acceptable in a country that is insistent that *we* are always wrong. We make ourselves small. We push through when we should rest. We hide our authentic selves under people-pleasing artifice. We suffer through moments of achievement soured by doubt. That is no way to live. It is bondage.

But we are living in revolutionary times. Transformation is coming—for you and me. In the summer of 2021, Simone Biles—winner of more Olympic and World Championship medals than any gymnast of her generation; the only person on Earth who can flip backward twice with enough power to twist three times in the air before her feet touch the ground; the GOAT, whom everyone was watching with anticipation— withdrew from several events in the Tokyo Olympics. She said she needed rest, physical and mental relief.[3] She stood firm in her decision even as she was publicly castigated, called a "selfish sociopath" and "national embarrassment" by commentators and keyboard warriors who had bought into the ever-potent narrative of the Mammy, believing that Black women are meant for the service of others and our personal needs and well-being do not matter.[4]

In a career full of one-of-a-kind moves, this was Biles at her most subversive. She prioritized herself and said no to a nation's expectations. And she sussed out the trick: acquiescence has never saved Black women. We might as well choose our full selves. We might as well stop studying our knees and look up. We might as well be healthy. We might as well be authentic. We might as well be big. We might as well be free.

Biles and Naomi Osaka, who pulled out of the French Open that same summer to focus on her mental health, have a lot of folks talking about the Black femme rebellion to come— sisters throwing off the shackles of other folks' expectations.[5]

Even the *Washington Post* crowed, "Black women, across generations, heed Biles' example."[6]

We can reject America's broken narrative about Black women. We can choose our own well-being, our own accomplishments, and our own joy. We can choose ourselves. But if Black women are going to get free and move from policing ourselves (and each other) to liberation, we need a plan.

Come on, there's room for everyone. And no one cares if your knees touch or not.

PART I

What Is Freedom?

CHAPTER 1

You Are Already Alright

You are at peace when you
don't need more or less—when you
don't need to be a king or a saint.

—RUMI

Say it with me:

I am alright.

You are alright.

We are alright.

And we will get free together.

Alrightness is not perfection. We all have flaws. (I am a grammar snob and a horrible procrastinator who cannot resist an impulse purchase.) Our flaws are not caused by Blackness or womanhood.

Alrightness is not aggrandizement. Mythology narrows Black women—obscures our souls and scars and beating hearts. I don't call my sisters "queens." I suppose some of our ancestors may have been royalty. I am comfortable saying that most were not. And I am certain that it doesn't matter, because monarchy is no antidote to racism and sexism and Black women don't need a shaky pedestal. We are not rulers over our sisters or brothers.

You and I come from the resilient ones who survived the death and despair of the Middle Passage.

We are the daughters of the women who had the foresight to braid seeds in their hair to make sure their people and their cultures would survive in a new land.[1]

We are the descendants of kitchen magicians who turned enslavers' scraps into culinary masterpieces.

We are the progeny of women who, sick and tired of being sick and tired, would not shut up or yield their seats.

We come from artisans who wove sisal and palm leaves into baskets, and songbirds who crooned arias and sang "Hound Dog" before Elvis ever swiveled his hips or Doja Cat offered her remix.[2]

But beyond all of that—above anything we have collectively accomplished, created, or survived—our simple existence is divine. It is no mistake. And the authentic ways we inhabit our skin and move and love and rage and fight and create and nurture and mourn add needed texture to the fabric of humanity. We are human beings navigating our lives against impressive odds as best we can. We are valuable in our imperfect perfection. We are neither innately damaged nor fundamentally flawed. We are alright.

Black women and girls are alright, yet we are the subject of constant critique, correction, and control, both from broader society and our own communities. We are told, implicitly and explicitly, that our natural appearance and inclinations are no good and need repair.

Bobos and Blue Ivy; Ladies and Loudies

Remember when folks started a Change.org petition decrying baby Blue Ivy's "matted dreads" and urging Beyonce and Jay-Z to "properly care for" their daughter's hair, which was just healthy kinky hair unrestrained by barrettes, beads, or bobos?[5] The Black community has folded a belief in Black femme physical inferiority into our culture such that beloved cultural rituals have developed around "fixing" Black girl hair when the occasion demands she be pretty. Saturday morning. Straightening combs. Heavy grease. Admonitions against "tender-headedness." The lesson: highly textured and coarse hair that displays more sheen than shine needs to be tamed and requires more extensive maintenance than any other. It doesn't. Kinks require special maintenance only if you are intent on prodding them into uniformity and styles meant for straight hair. But too many of us are convinced that Black hair is "problem hair," especially on Black women, and that wraps and weaves and wigs are not just fun ways to play with style, but necessary tools to hide physical defects.

In a 2007 study called "Ladies or Loudies?" Dr. Edward W. Morris, a sociologist from the University of Kentucky, found that teachers at a Kentucky middle school subjected Black girls to unique discipline directed at perceptions of them as aggressive, loud, and not ladylike.[4] (Accusations that just happen to align with traits enslavers assigned to African women to justify bondage and assault.) Most of the educators at the school Morris studied were Black women, who told researchers they were trying to teach Black girls life skills because they "don't get [these skills] at home," or "their parents are unemployed a lot of times," or "there is a lack of a male figure in the home." (Assumptions that mirror biased negative beliefs about Black families.) When it came to Black girls, educators encouraged bodily control, quietness, and passivity over more assertive behaviors that were subtly encouraged in White middle-class children.

Morris discovered that while Black girls at the school dominated class discussions, actively participated in class, competed for opportunities, and stood up for others, they were not rewarded for their effort. Educators actually stifled outspokenness that supports academic success in order to teach Black girls to be more ladylike.

This distorted lens has contributed to Black girls being demonized and pushed out of school through disproportionate suspensions and expulsions, and disproportionately disciplined and treated violently not just in Kentucky, but nationwide. Overpolicing of Black girls in schools has resulted in them being the fastest-growing group in juvenile detention nationwide.

Black femmes are lied to from the day we are born—sold distortions of who we are and who we should be that separate us from our authentic selves and cloak our divinity. Is it any wonder that it is hard for Black women and girls to hold on to an awareness of our alrightness when, in the face of misogynoir, we are forced to make adjustments to the way we show up in the world to help ensure our safety and access to opportunity, to protect and provide for our families, and to advance our communities? Is it any wonder that when I asked nearly fifty Black women if they felt free, 60 percent said they did not?

Like a Forty-Five-Year-Old White Man

A friend of mine has a saying she uses to describe walking into a room with confidence and a belief that your authentic self is owed respect and regard. She'll say, "Girl, I'm 'bout to walk into that room like a forty-five-year-old straight White man."

In America, Whiteness and maleness are identities associated with value, intelligence, attractiveness, leadership, and competence. White men are not evaluated negatively for traits associated with their race or gender. By contrast, since Europeans began marauding, African-descended peoples have been noted as inferior, stupid, untrustworthy, childlike, ugly, and animalistic. Across cultures, women have been branded unclean, seductive, scheming, and guileful. These traits have been used to justify our servitude and subjugation for centuries and have made it so that when Black women and girls enter a room people often see us as problems in need of a solution. We must weigh each encounter and experience to mind that we are showing up the "right" way, obscuring the things about us that we have been told are bad.

Are my frizzy edges laid enough? Am I deferential enough? Am I confident? Too confident? Is my voice too loud? Are my clothes too bright? Should I tell them that I am a single mom? Is my ass too phat? (Will folks at work sexualize me?) Is my ass too fat? (Will my doctor blame every ailment on my weight?) Am I not educated or credentialed enough? Am I too educated and credentialed to be a good romantic partner to a man? What's that sister over there doing? Is she showing up right? If she shows up wrong, what will people think of me?

Laura, whom you will meet in chapter 7, talked to me about how her body has been problematized throughout her life. As an adolescent she heard from well-meaning family that she was "developing too much" and becoming "too curvy." This is not uncommon for Black girls. The National Women's Law Center reports that "Black girls are more likely to be disciplined for clothing at school than their peers, because 'adults see them as older and more sexual.'"[5]

At school and, in Laura's experience, at work. Laura says that when she entered the work world, she noticed that the pencil skirts and cute tops that were an acceptable, stylish uniform for her White colleagues were appraised differently on her frame.

"I was told that I should probably watch what I wear. You know, dress for success," she says. "My body doesn't look the way the hierarchy in front of me looks. And I was conscious of the fact that no one was talking to the White women I worked with about how their bodies look—only me."

Sister, you and I can never truly "walk into a room like a for-ty-five-year-old straight White man." A White man may walk into a job interview fretting about his skills and references, but he won't have to expend energy worrying about whether the way the hair grows from his head is unprofessional or whether his body in his suit will read like an invitation.

Self-evaluation is a real and necessary part of being a member of a marginalized community. You and I know that Black women and girls are often judged harshly and rarely given the benefit of the doubt or second chances, and so we adjust. But exposure to society's negative perceptions often, over time, moves us to see ourselves as problems, too. There is a difference—sometimes a mere sliver of a difference—between strategically responding to the realities of racism and sexism in society and buying into and enforcing racist and sexist beliefs.

Black women and girls will not be free as long as we embrace a racist society's belief that we are fatally flawed and remain complicit in enforcing that belief on our sisters and our daughters. We get to the promised land only if we can access our full humanity and acknowledge our inherent value while leaving room for complication. We can get free only once we recognize our inherent alrightness.

A Recipe for Liberation

This is not a yoga book. But yoga has been a critical part of my freedom journey. It is the seed from which this book grew, and I share some of the principles that have been most trans-formative to me in this book.

In 2020, as the world was falling apart, I decided I wanted to become a certified yoga teacher—thick thighs and all. I studied anatomy, breathing, meditation, and how to properly place my hands and feet on the mat, and I immersed myself in the philosophy and texts of yoga practice: the Bhagavad Gita, the Upanishads, the *Mahabharata*, and, of course, the foun-dational *Yoga Sutras* with its transformational opening lines:

> *Now, the teachings of yoga.*
>
> *Yoga is to still the patterning of consciousness.*
>
> *Then pure awareness can abide in its very nature.*
>
> *Otherwise, awareness takes itself to be the patterns of consciousness.*

Patanjali, author of the sutras, believed there is a defect in human understanding. We are divine beings observing a human experience—pure awareness. The problem is that we mistake ourselves for all the feelings and thoughts and experiences that swirl around us each day. It is only when we can still our consciousness, perhaps through meditation or matching our breath to movements, that we can understand our true nature and relieve ourselves of human pain and suffering.

Studying this, I had an epiphany: Does this not explain something of the Black femme experience, too? Sister, we are souls working to realize our true nature through the noise of misogyny, racism, and other oppressions. The eight limbs of yoga offer a roadmap for humans to reach enlightenment and realize their essential natures. I believe there is a pathway for Black femme liberation. We can get free by intentionally decolonizing our minds to cultivate an unshakeable belief in Black women and girls' alrightness.

Part II of this book explores six pillars of Black femme freedom:

- **Spot the distortions.** Black women must learn to see distorted beliefs about us and to recognize the ways they are maintained by broader society and our communities. And we must teach future generations to do the same. Lisa, whom you will meet in chapter 9, likens this to learning to identify poison before it enters your bloodstream and threatens your well-being.

- **Know your truth.** We can locate our authentic selves outside of society's distorted beliefs about Black women and girls, unhooking our authentic selves from caricatures crafted to abet human bondage, White supremacy, and patriarchy.

- **Celebrate the real you.** We can learn to accept and celebrate our authentic selves, even the benign traits we have been told are bad: our sex lives, singleness, natural hair, or courage to speak up and advocate for ourselves.

- **Understand the cost of liberation.** We can determine how much we are willing to "pay" to inhabit spaces where our authentic selves might be unsafe or unwelcome. For instance, is that high-paying corporate job worth the ways you must sacrifice your identity to fit in? There is no wrong response, but a free Black woman must know the answer.

- **Practice freedom.** Liberation is not so much a destination as a sustained practice of choosing our individual highest good again and again. We can cultivate a freedom practice designed to center our alrightness and keep our well-being top of mind.

- **See free Black women everywhere.** Rooted in our own Black femme freedom, we can learn to see and nurture the freedom of other Black women and girls.

If Black women can do this and teach our daughters to do this, too, we can unlock our full power and walk into any room honoring our highest authentic selves—even if no one else does. We can more clearly love ourselves, prioritize ourselves, and secure our mental, emotional, and spiritual well-being in the face of external forces. We can advocate for ourselves and our sisters—a form of self-love and self-care in itself. We can live lives of abundance and joy.

This would be monumental.

CHAPTER 2

I Wish I Knew How It Would Feel to Be Free

*She had not known the
weight until she felt the freedom!*

—NATHANIEL HAWTHORNE

I feel free when I am in the company of my sister friends. Like when we gathered to celebrate my fiftieth birthday at a charming little cabin in the woods of Brown County, Indiana. Maybelle's Cabin has big, comfy beds, an old record player with a dusty collection of LPs, two miniature horses, a pair of friendly Labradors, chickens, a hot tub, a fireplace, and a nearby diner that serves Appalachian fare, like big buttery biscuits and bourbon-infused everything. My girls and I supplied the laughter and, as my friend Carolyn would say, "foolishment." Oh, it was joyous! That weekend, writing in front of the fireplace, sipping moonshine in the hot tub, and cackling at copious amounts of cutting up by my besties, I felt a peace I can experience only with other Black women. It is the freedom of not having to explain, justify, or apologize for any damn thing about my Black woman self—not my night bonnet or vernacular or cultural rituals, like rubbing my feet with raw shea butter to protect them against the drying fall air. (No excuse for ashiness, even on a weekend retreat!) These women are a mirror that affirms my authentic self and my alrightness.

I feel free when I am engaging in creative expression, especially when I write about Black women and girls, amplifying our lives and experiences. There is magic in making the invisible visible.

I feel free when I am engaged in spiritual practice—when, in the silence of the early morning, I steal away to my home office, light some incense, and settle onto my meditation cushion; when I swing my arms over my head, reaching toward heaven during sun salutations; when I hear the swell of the gospel song "Total Praise" or the funky beat drop of Londrelle's "Hare Krishna Mahamantra."

If we want to live life as free Black women, we have to define what liberation means. You can't use a GPS without having a destination in mind. Sister, to understand your personal definition of liberation, it is useful to explore the moments when you feel most free. Who is there? (Who is not?) How do you show up? Why do you feel unshackled in those moments?

There are ways that you will experience freedom that are intensely personal and informed by your unique story.

There are also elements of liberation that feel nearly universal. "I Wish I Knew How It Would Feel to Be Free," written by jazz man Billy Taylor, became an anthem of the civil rights movement for the vivid way it captured the yearning for emancipation. Freedom to speak out. Freedom to love. Freedom to be seen. Freedom to live. Freedom to soar. Listening to Nina Simone's famous cover of the song, I found that the songwriter's idea of freedom is not so far from mine. When I feel free it is because I am affirmed, allowed my voice and choices, and spiritually connected.

While writing this book, I interviewed or surveyed more than fifty women. I asked almost all of them to share their idea of Black femme freedom. There were several singular responses. Taylor, a twenty-something, tired of the insistence that Black women be twice as good to get half as much, offered, "The freedom to not be is just as important as the freedom to be. Black women should be free to struggle, to be mediocre, or not be the very best." Alycia said that freedom is "the grace to make mistakes and learn from them and not be defined by them." Natasha defined freedom as "owning land and living off the land as much as possible." One anonymous respondent offered, sadly, "I don't know. I'm not sure I've seen it." But the Black women I spoke to overwhelmingly defined liberation in five ways: having financial security, unimpeded access to opportunity, support in focusing on physical and emotional wellness, affirmation of their identities, and freedom of choice.

It makes sense that many women would name financial security as a foundation for freedom. Too many of us don't have it. In an issue brief titled "Rejecting Business as Usual: Improving Employment Outcomes and Economic Security for Black Women," the National Partnership for Women and Families reports that "the challenges and barriers that Black women confront—in terms of wage disparities, lack of supports for caregiving, over-concentration in jobs with low pay and few benefits, and perpetually having their work devalued—mirror the challenges that many women experience on the job, but often are harsher due to the complex mix of attitudes, stereotypes, and biases that shape workplace culture."[1] Nearly 19 percent of us live in poverty.[2] At the same time, Black women are most likely to be the primary sources of support for their families.[3] That leaves many of us trapped in unfulfilling and toxic situations. "Personal freedom is having the resources to leave an unhealthy job environment, an unhealthy relationship, or any physical place that does not honor or respect my well-being," explains Dionne.

In response to the pressure Black women face to prioritize other people's needs and neglect their own, several women said freedom would mean the ability to focus on their own emotional and physical wellness. Imagine if Black women could do that. And if, as a woman named Nicole dreamed, Black women had access to "adequate healthcare and doctors who listen because they actually live by their Hippocratic oath and see me as a human being." How different might our health outcomes be? Perhaps we would not disproportionately die in childbirth.[4] Maybe one in four of us would not be diabetic.[5] Our depression might not so often be overlooked.[6]

Many women shared their wish to be liberated from the things, such as financial instability and poor-quality healthcare, that often stand in the way of our opportunity and success. Taylor wants to know that "no matter where I am in life or where I want to go, there's nothing holding me back—systemically, structurally, or even mentally."

Nearly all of the women I asked about liberation expressed the need to have their identities affirmed as an element of freedom. Chafing at constant critique and admonitions to fix herself, Diane says, "The ability to show up as my authentic self in any space positively affects my confidence and releases me from the shackles of societal expectations. To me it's important that I'm able to wear my hair in any state that I want, to freely express my personality through my clothing choices, to incorporate African American vernacular English in my speech and not have to constantly code-switch, to challenge authority and the people around me when their perspectives are limited, and to be as extra and loud or as quiet and subdued as I want to be without concern for how other people are perceiving me or judging me."

More than anything else, Black women told me that they define freedom as the ability to choose. Black women want to be free to decide how we show up and how we live. We want what the US Constitution tells us is the God-given, unalienable right of all human beings to life, liberty, and the pursuit of happiness.

"[I want to] free myself from the expectations of Blackness and womanhood and be deeply connected to myself as spirit and to who God created," says Camike. "Then I get to decide how I will navigate the world as a Black person and as a Black woman. I choose what that means for me. The world does not get to determine who I am. I am free to explore the vastness of the Black experience. Regarding womanhood, I am free to explore masculine and feminine—to be strong or weak, vulnerable [or] assertive, loud or silent, to lead or be led. I am free to choose or just be still."

The Absence of Choices

The reality for us, sister, is that we cannot always control our access to the things we associate with freedom. Many of us work hard yet still lack financial security. Our history means generational wealth is too rare in Black families. We face numerous structural barriers to success—racism and patriarchy chief among them. We seldom see our identities affirmed or celebrated in this country that voraciously consumes Black culture and swag but disdains the folks they come from. Box braids and big booties are considered cute on Kardashians but low-class on Keesha. Black women and girls are decidedly not supported in prioritizing our mental and physical well-being, and every indication reveals that the broken American healthcare system certainly does not value us. Misogynoir and the self-regulation that it demands often rob Black women and girls of the power to simply choose what comes naturally or what is best for us and those we love. We are in constant negotiation with America's biased views of race and gender. It feels disempowering and oppressive.

But we can still be free.

Nearly every Black woman's response to "What is freedom?" can be distilled to one thing: freedom of choice. We want financial security so we are free to choose. We want structural barriers removed so we are free to choose. We want to be affirmed in choosing how we show up as Black people, women, and our other intersected identities. We want to make decisions that support our health. We want to choose ourselves, our families, and our lives without judgment or punishment. Anything else is bondage. In her work *Feminist Theory: From Margin to Center*, feminist scholar bell hooks wrote, "Being oppressed means the absence of choices."

Choice is freedom. And, sister, we can have it.

There are warriors working every day to dismantle systemic racism and patriarchy and cure the sicknesses they have created. But it is slow going. The work has already taken hundreds of years and counting. I doubt the world will get shed of these oppressions in my lifetime. The world we have been given is imperfect. All we can do is choose how we show up in it.

I am writing this book, my sister, so that you and I can see ourselves more clearly and value ourselves more fully; so we can navigate the realities of racism, sexism, and other oppressions, making the sometimes hard and punishing choices they require from a place of strength and freedom, preferencing our needs. Like sister Simone Biles did when she told the folks who wanted her emotional and physical labor at the Olympics: not today.

If Black women and girls can learn this, then we will know what it feels like to be free.

CHAPTER 3

Freedom Rituals

*Caring for myself is not self-indulgence,
it is self-preservation, and that is an act
of political warfare.*

—AUDRE LORDE

On the morning that I finished this chapter, I woke up at 5 a.m. I did an ayurvedic morning routine. I took my medicine and a tablespoon of collagen (so my skin can stay not cracking). I lit some incense and turned on my favorite playlist. I did some yoga stretches and sun salutations on my mat. I performed some self-reiki. And I meditated. This is a ritual that makes me feel good. It is a ritual that I had not performed in months.

By the time this book is published, it will have been two years since my husband was diagnosed with frontotemporal dementia. It is a monstrous disease that has forced me to say goodbye too soon to the man who knew all the words to the seventies soft-rock cheesefest "Please Come to Boston"; my favorite road trip companion; the guy who knew a billion animal facts and could identify a bird in flight from a car doing seventy-five down the highway; the expert deep sea fisherman; the movie night companion who quoted lines from *Tombstone* and *Monty Python and the Holy Grail* with me; the reader who devoured every new James Patterson book; the earnest but inept do-it-yourselfer who built me a pergola on the back deck, because I wanted one (it was rickety but lovely); my biggest cheerleader, who sometimes embarrassed me with how hard he would push folks to buy my first book; the former Navy guy who really wanted us to take a cruise so he could show me how the sky looks at night in the middle of the ocean (we never got around to that). This disease has turned me from wife to caretaker. It is messy, frightening, and heartbreaking—the hardest thing I have ever endured.

Months after my husband's diagnosis, I took on a new job that felt like a once-in-a-lifetime opportunity. I became president of a midwestern women's fund that makes grants to women- and girl-serving organizations and advocates for women and girls in my community. I spent more than a decade raging about gender biases and inequities. Now, I have an opportunity to confront those things and change them. I am excited every day that I get to do this. It is inspiring work. It is rewarding work. It is also hard work. I am advocating for support in an environment where women and girls receive only 2 percent of all US philanthropic dollars[1] and in a state with a D average on the "Status of Women in the States" report card from the Institute for Women's Policy Research.[2] And I am conscious of being part of a sharp evolution in not-for-profit leadership, and women's fund leadership specifically, since 2020. Fifty-one percent of place-based women's funds are now led by women of color, 73 percent of those by Black women.[3] But reports show that new leaders of color receive less support than their White counterparts while facing great expectations and significant challenges, often including the burden of being one of few or the first to hold their positions. When you are the first, there is tremendous pressure not to be the last.[4] As a *RuPaul's Drag Race* fan, I have, more than once as I navigated this new role, thought of the legendary queen's words before each episode's final lip-sync battle between contestants: "Good luck. And don't fuck it up!" I refuse to fuck this up. This work is too important.

I did not think of my new job or my caretaking when my publisher agreed to partner on this book. I was simply elated that I could talk to my sisters and share my thoughts on how we get free. *I can do this*, I thought. I can take care of a chronically ill spouse, run an organization, write a book, sit on several boards, be a daughter, be a bonus mom, be a friend, be an active member of my sorority and other organizations. I can fulfill all of my chosen and unchosen responsibilities. You know how we do.

So many Black women are overwhelmed with passion and vision and ambition. We want things for ourselves, our families, our communities. We may need more resources. We may need more support. Even the most privileged of us usually do. But we do the things anyway. Defiantly. Hopefully. I love that about us. But, too often, in our doing, serving, and achieving, we sacrifice the most important thing: our own well-being.

More than halfway into writing this book about Black women and liberation, I realized I was doing just that.

I would vow to wake up early and complete my thirty-minute morning ritual. I would pledge to find time to move my body, to breathe, to meditate, to cook a healthy meal, to practice my writing craft, to read, to connect with friends and family—things that make me whole and healthy. I would begin each day with the best of intentions for taking care of myself, and then I would shove my promises to myself aside in favor of doing, serving, and achieving. And then I squeezed in easier and less thoughtful ways of self-soothing: doomscrolling, binge-watching, and eating. It left me depleted and disappointed because I was not keeping the commitments I made to myself. I felt chained to other people's expectations of me. I was writing a book about Black women and liberation and was feeling mighty unfree.

Sister, we cannot be free unless we believe we deserve it. *Really* believe. We have to believe that we deserve autonomy and that our bodies, our minds, and our souls are worthy of regard and care. We do not exist simply for achievement or serving others or disproving lies about Black folks or women. We are valuable in our very existence. (We are alright!) Yes, there are things worth sacrificing for—people we love, world-changing causes, communities in need, our own ambition. For Black women, this is especially true. But we cannot sustain any work caring for others if we are broken. Our achievements mean nothing if we are dead.

Sister, we must believe that our well-being is most important. How can we get to liberation if we believe our needs come after everyone else's? We have to love ourselves first. That's the thing. We have to love ourselves most of all and treat our minds and bodies accordingly.

I invite you, as you read this book, to consider a practice of self-love. Because self-love is foundational to liberation.

This chapter outlines some ways you can honor yourself while reading this book and after. Do these things. Introduce them slowly. Make them habits. Make and keep commitments to yourself. In the next section of the book, I'll offer some ways to leverage these habits on your freedom journey.

Create Your Own Morning Ritual

I move differently when I honor my commitment to my morning ritual—even when I do it hastily or have to meditate in my car in the parking lot before walking into the office. (Not ideal, but better than nothing.) I feel calmer and more centered. And I feel loved by the most important person in my life: *me*.

English author and poet Doreen Valiente called rituals "acts of love and pleasure." With what act of love and pleasure can you begin your day? Maybe you sip tea and watch thirty minutes of an old favorite sitcom. Maybe you read a passage from *Daily Bread* and pray. Maybe you give your body a loving massage with fragrant oil when you step from the shower. Maybe you hug your baby tight, inhaling deep that intoxicating infant smell. Maybe you sit on your porch and watch the world wake up. Maybe you do a crossword puzzle. Maybe you shut yourself in the bathroom and enjoy five minutes of silence before the day comes flying at you.

Whatever you do, treat the moment as sacred. Be intentional. Try to create a pleasing environment. (I burn incense and candles.) And be *present*. This morning routine, whether five minutes or fifty, could be the only time you have for yourself in a day. Savor it. And before you move on, take a moment to practice gratitude that you can feel and express love for yourself.

You likely already have a morning *routine*—actions you perform by rote to start your day. I am simply asking you to intentionally introduce something sweet to your regimen. Make your first choice every day *you*. Begin the day by loving on your free Black woman self.

Detox

As Black women, we are inundated with toxic inputs about our identity. It has always been so. There have always been prejudiced government reports about our lives, sermons meant to put us in our places, and art that erases us while elevating other women as examples of beauty and femininity. But more than ever the negativity seems unavoidable, especially on social media, which feeds on anger and argument, outrage and distraction. Misogynoir is constantly amplified across social media channels—even simply in the sharing to disagree. There is a market for devaluing Black women and critiquing our appearance and choices under the guise of serving up "truth" or "teaching us" to be better. (Cough . . . Kevin Samuels . . . cough. Merchants of misogynoir always bring to mind a line from "People Get Ready," the classic song by The Impressions: "There ain't no room for the hopeless sinner, who will hurt all [Black wo]mankind, just to save his own [ego and fragile masculinity].")

Stereotypes of Black women are all over the place—comedy stand-up, drive-time radio, Black celebrity forums, reality TV, and scripted TV. Sometimes we all want to shut off our brains and sink into some trashy entertainment without caring about sociopolitical issues. I get it. But it is because we so often shut off our brains as we watch reality TV, scroll social media, or listen to the hip-hop top 40 that the messages we find there can be so insidious.

There is something particularly twisted about being entertained by your own oppression. And no group is asked to do that quite like Black women are. The tiny cuts of subtle sexism and racism are weathering. They leave us bloody and exhausted.

Consider the media you consume regularly. How many reinforcements of stereotypes do you find there? Would you subject someone you love to repeated insults and disingenuous critique? Are you addicted to outrage over the things people say about us? Are you more drawn to negativity about Black women than positivity?

Do me a favor, sister. While you are reading this book and embarking on your journey to freedom, I'd like you to detox from any media that regularly malign or reduce Black women to stereotypes.

After you are done with this book, you may find that some of the old things that entertained you no longer do. Or, you may decide, as an old feminist friend used to say, "Fuck it! I like it!" But if you decide to return to those things, you can do so in freedom with new awareness and a new ability to extract yourself from the distorted images you find there.

And you may find yourself yearning for a more important sort of detox, removing institutions and people from your life that do not treat you well, who judge Black women and girls harshly and play Devil's advocate with our humanity. When you are truly free, it is hard to abide by anyone intent on seeing you enslaved.

Nourish

Replace negative inputs with positive ones. Sister, I invite you while reading this book to consciously consume things that support your growth, health, and well-being.

Spend time with the people who embrace the authentic you, who make you smile. Seek wise counsel from those who encourage you to be your best. Rest in spaces that open your heart, where you can remove your mask and just be. Do things that bring you joy. Color with your granddaughter. Dance. Put your toes in some grass.

I recently discovered a charming little park near my house with mature trees bending over a cool creek and a real flowing artesian well. It feels like someplace sacred and hidden, even if it is just off a busy suburban road. It is a happy place where I can dip my toes in the water, lean back, and look up into the trees. Find your happy place and drink it in.

Listen to music that uplifts and poetry that is affirming. Read the literary greats: bell hooks. Audre Lorde. Toni

Morrison. Alice Walker. Read Lucille Clifton's "Won't You Celebrate with Me?" and then read it again. Listen to Mahalia Jackson confess "How I Got Over," then hear Queen Bey declare "You won't break my soul." Focus on ideas that make you smarter and help you know the world more fully. Consume work that inspires—that makes you bigger and better rather than smaller and more embattled.

And don't forget your body.

When I am most consumed with doing, serving, and achieving, I am not intentional about my physical health. I will skip breakfast because I have to make it to an 8 a.m. meeting. I will eat a late, too-heavy lunch at the office (sugar, salt, and fat are attractive addictions on a stressful day). I come home exhausted after a long commute and longer workday; order DoorDash, including dessert, instead of cooking; have a glass of wine (or two); and fall into bed. I hit the snooze button in the morning ('cause wine), too tired to hit the gym or work in that morning ritual. Rinse. Repeat. I give my body enough to convince it to get up and do stuff in the short term without considering the long-term repercussions. Maybe you are like me.

The diet industry has convinced us that health is only about what we *don't* put in our bodies (gluten, calories, meat, etc.). Sister, while you are reading this book, center on abundance and nourish your body with all the good stuff you can. Eat some dark, leafy greens. Drink water. Give your body movement: dance or walk around the block or try a short yoga flow on YouTube.

When you fill yourself up with good fuel and habits, there is less room for less useful things. Be nourished.

Breathe

We rarely pay attention to respiration—the thing keeping us alive—until we find ourselves breathless. Now that we have seen millions die, gasping for air. Now that we have reckoned with ventilator shortages. Now that we have masked to keep from breathing in the wrong thing. Now that we have watched a man die, struggling to breathe and calling for his mother, under a police officer's knee. We know this thing better than ever before: breath is life.

Breathing is part of the autonomic nervous system that regulates involuntary bodily functions, such as heart rate, blood pressure, digestion, and sexual arousal. It delivers life-giving oxygen to our cells and helps expel waste gases. Sometimes, when we are stressed or anxious, we can unconsciously disrupt this process. Tensed at our computers watching tweets from red pill pontificators, we breathe shallowly. Walking alone in a parking garage late at night, we breathe harder. We lie in bed on a Sunday night, ruminating on our mile-long task list and we hyperventilate. Even in the best of times, we often forget to take deep, cleansing breaths that fill our lungs and cause our bellies to rise, followed by long, slow, calming exhales.

My favorite poem about the Black femme experience, "The Bridge Poem" by Donna Kate Rushin, includes this memorable line from a Black woman to all those grasping for her service and labor:

I am sick
Of having to remind you

To breathe
Before you suffocate
Your own fool self

Mind that you are not so busy reminding other folks to breathe that you suffocate your own fool self. Sister, I invite you to become conscious of your breath while reading this book.

A good place to start is simply noticing your breathing. Do you breathe differently when you are relaxed and happy versus when you are under stress? See how you breathe when sitting in nature and how you breathe sitting in front of the TV watching the 11 o'clock news. In an article in *Forbes* magazine, Charlotte Mulloy, a Colorado-based psychotherapist at Freespira, a digital breathwork therapy company, offered, "Intentional breaks during our day, even if it's just two minutes of noticing, 'Hey, I'm breathing,' can actually soothe your body in ways you didn't even know you needed."

You may also consider making ten minutes of conscious breathing part of your everyday morning ritual:

1. Inhale through your nose.

2. Let the air inflate your belly and chest.

3. Keep your chest open: shoulders away from your ears and shoulder blades reaching toward each other.

4. Maintain a rhythm, not breathing too deeply or shallowly.

I discovered breathwork in yoga teacher training. It is one of the eight foundational pillars of yoga practice. *Pranayama*, the Sanskrit word for breathwork, can be translated as "breath restraint" or "freedom of breath," and it includes a variety of techniques that support physical, mental, and emotional healing. Once you know these exercises, they can help you soothe yourself, find calm, lift depression, stay alert, and achieve better focus. You may consider adding some of these breathing techniques to aid in your liberation journey. (See the box "Transformative Breathing" at the end of the chapter.)

Focus

You have to be *present* to be free. Aware. Tuned in. Woke. When we move mindlessly, we are more susceptible to distorted images of Black womanhood and detached from our own existence and experience. We must be present in our bodies to know what makes us feel good and to read the signals when something is going wrong. If we are mindless, we do not know if we are taking life-giving breaths or barely sustaining gasps. We must be present in our minds to identify how negative biases about Black women have crept into our thinking about ourselves and our sisters. When we are disconnected, we often miss how we are complicit in our sisters' oppression. Alas, we are a distracted society, constantly harassed by text notifications and pop-ups and multitasking.

Meditation is practice for mindfulness that presents an opportunity to learn to be present, using focused concentration to bring yourself back to the present moment again and

again. Contrary to popular belief, meditation is not about elim-
inating all thoughts. It is instead about becoming an observer
of the moment. It is about listening, about making space and
creating silence for the still small voice of the universe—of
the soul.

Alice Walker—writer, thinker, Buddhist, icon—has said
she loves meditation "because that's where you find what your
voice is. You cannot really find it easily in this culture. This cul-
ture is the noisiest culture ever, ever. I think the damage that
it has done to people is in that realm of silencing them. They
are overwhelmed by gadgets. They don't know what to think
because they're so heavily programmed about what it is that
they should want and should think."

Meditation is a proven technique for reducing stress, anx-
iety, and depression; lowering blood pressure; strengthening
the immune system; improving memory; helping with addic-
tion; improving sleep; and more. It is an important part of my
morning ritual and my spiritual practice—time to, as Walker
has said, "steal back myself."

Start a meditation practice while reading this book. You
needn't sit for long periods of time or do anything compli-
cated. Breathwork and watching the breath can serve as an
easy meditation. And here is another approach: Find a space
to sit without distractions. Sit comfortably on the floor, on a
meditation cushion, or on a chair. Set a timer. Straighten your
back and let your hands rest in your lap, palms up or down.
Breathe. As you exhale, release all the tension in your mus-
cles. Do a scan of your body, from head to toe, to see where
you may be holding stress. Find a natural rhythm with your

breath. Now, just sit. Just be. Your mind will wander, especially when you are new to meditation practice. When yours wanders off, simply bring it back to the moment. Doing this for just five minutes a day can be transformative.

Bear Witness

Keeping a journal has long been recognized as an effective way to help achieve goals, track progress and growth, gain self-confidence, reduce stress and anxiety, and find inspiration. Make a commitment to chronicle your freedom journey by journaling.

You may want to mark the evolution of your self-care practices. How do you feel, for instance, after meditating for the first time? How do you feel after a month of sustained practice? Perhaps you want to write down the discoveries you make about yourself. What negative ideas about your humanity have cemented in your psyche? Maybe you keep a list of nourishing literature and music and podcasts.

Journaling can be as simple or complicated as you like. You may find a pretty journal and buy a set of fancy colored pens and stencils to make your liberation log special. (This is totally something I would do.) Or maybe you just want to tap your feelings into the Notes app on your iPhone. The method isn't important; the doing is.

Remember, liberation is a practice and not a destination. Writing about your journey gives you something to return to when the road is rough. Similarly, it can give you a roadmap to share with other women yearning to be free.

Positive Podcasts to Feed Your Mind

The Hey Girl Podcast (Alex Elle)   Created with sisterhood and storytelling in mind, in this podcast author Alex Elle sits down with people who inspire her. No new episodes are posting, but there's a great roster of old interviews.

Black Girl's Guide to Surviving Menopause (Omisade Burney-Scott)   This curated intergenerational exchange is a space for exploration, mentorship, intimacy, and vulnerability around life, identity, and change.

Finding Refuge (Michelle Cassandra Johnson)   This podcast emerged from work based on the exploration of collective grief and liberation. It exists to remind us about all the ways we can find refuge during unsettling and uncertain times, and to remind us about the resilience that comes from allowing ourselves to find refuge.

Wiser Than Me (Julia Louis-Dreyfus)   The actress wondered why the hell we don't hear more from older women, and so sat down with legends like Isabel Allende, Jane Fonda, Diane von Furstenberg, Carol Burnett, and Fran Lebowitz to get schooled on how to live a full and meaningful life.

"I Choose Me" Playlist

- "Morning Asana" by Londrelle
- "Activation Affirmations from the Collective" by Bliss Looper and Activation
- "Inner Peace" by Beautiful Chorus
- "Healing" by Sampa the Great
- "Petal" by Raveena
- "The View" by DAO featuring Adam Friedman
- "There She Is Again" by Leah Free
- "I Release" by Beautiful Chorus
- "Know That You Are Loved" by Cleo Soul
- "A Beautiful Prayer" by Lizzy Jeff, Paola Jean, and Mama Diivinity

Transformative Breathing

Diaphragm Breathing

- **Benefits:** Relaxation; lower blood pressure and heart rate; improved muscle function during exercise
- **How to do it:** Lie down flat on your back. You may use a pillow underneath your head and knees for comfort. Place

a hand on your upper chest and another on your belly, beneath your rib cage. Breathe in slowly through your nose, allowing air to expand the belly, pushing it up against your hand, while the chest remains still. Breathe out and let the stomach deflate while you exhale through pursed lips. The chest continues to remain still.

- **Duration:** Try for five to ten minutes.

Four-Square or Box Breathing

- **Benefits:** Relieves stress; reduces symptoms of anxiety and depression; improves focus and cognitive function

- **How to do it:** Breathe in for a count of four. Hold air in your lungs for a count of four. Exhale for a count of four. Hold your lungs empty for the same count.

- **Duration:** Try three to five rounds of box breathing

PART II

The Practice of Liberation

CHAPTER 4

Spot the Distortions

Many of us begin to put too much
value on how we are seen by others.
That's if we are seen at all.

—MEGAN THEE STALLION

There is a pillow in my living room, resting awkwardly on the wide brown leather chair next to the fireplace. I am looking at it as I write. I often do. Because the pillow explains everything about distorted views of Black women and men.

I bought it on a trip to Atlanta to promote my first book. After an event at the Hammonds House Museum, I wandered into the gift shop. (I can't resist a museum gift shop. Ever.) The pillow was the first thing to catch my eye. On one side is a black silhouette of Miriam Makeba, South African civil rights activist, ambassador, singer, actress, and songwriter also known as Mama Africa. On the other side is a quote from her: "The conqueror writes history. They came, they conquered, they wrote. Now, you don't expect people who came to invade us to write the truth about us. They will always write negative things about us and they have to do that because they have to justify their invasion."

I feel Makeba's words in my soul.

Our African foremothers were women with loves and hopes and practices and values and spirituality and knowledge and ways of being that were valid and deserved regard. Then they were kidnapped and hauled across the deadly Middle Passage to slavery in America.

In America, it would not do for Black women to have sovereignty over their own existence. We could not be divine beings. America needed Mammy—the willing servant without her own needs and desires. America needed Jezebel—sexually available for the entertainment of men and the breeding of new human property. America needed Sapphire—the snapping beast, mentally and physically able to carry any pain or burden. America needed the Matriarch—without the ability to adequately love children, partners, and family who might be killed or sold away, never to be seen again. The humanity of Black women, never mind our divinity, was inconvenient to enslavers and colonizers in a fledgling country that needed our foremothers as grease for its economic engine.

America had to lie about Black women to take away our freedom and justify the inhumanity of American chattel slavery. Black women were cast as sexually voracious and unrapeable sirens. Black women were called unnaturally strong and resilient; and aggressive, angry, snarling, snapping things. Black women were believed to be indifferent and heartless mothers and partners. Black women were deemed built for servitude and burden—the mules of the world, to borrow a phrase from sister Zora Neale Hurston.

The conqueror manufactured these distortions and then wrote them, enshrining them in literature, law, culture, and custom. It told the lies over and over again and for long after chattel slavery ended in 1865. And because America still needs to cover its sins by distorting Black women into twisted, monstrous things, it is still lying today. Not in the same ways. Hatred of Black women—misogynoir—is like water. It flows to fill its vessel.

Today, the lies are present in school dress codes that disproportionately punish Black girls for having bodies that are sexually "distracting." They are the foundation of how Black women and girls are overpoliced and incarcerated. They are woven into reality TV shows, cast and edited to highlight grown-ass Black women yanking weaves and throwing drinks at each other. They are front and center in Ronald Reagan's enduring "welfare queen" rhetoric that labels Black women conniving, irresponsible, man-repelling, constantly breeding, bad mothers. They are hiding behind the elevation of biracial, light-skinned, and non-Black women in advertising, beauty media, and music videos at the expense of brown-skinned women with tightly coiled hair and broader features. They are in the medical establishment's competing disinterest and revulsion at Black women's bodies—healthy or sick. They underpin Black male–led podcast conversations about Black women as romantic partners who need to learn their "place" as women.

Distortions of Black women's humanity have unfortunately even been accepted by those who should know better—people who claim to love Black women, like mothers, fathers, spiritual advisors, and community leaders. How could they not be? Our communities are part of American culture. To ask Black folks not to absorb any of the biases present in the larger culture is like asking a person not to breathe the air outside her front door.

Too many of Black women's alleged allies fail to question the broken values of a society steeped in oppression and White patriarchy. Some Black women are sexually adventurous. Some are angry. Some are workhorses. Some are single mothers. We are all and none of these things. Like everybody else, again, we are human. (What is wrong, really, with a woman who is angry—especially if she has endured the Black woman's history in America? What is wrong with a woman who enjoys sensual pleasures? How does a woman who raises her child alone carry more blame than a man who left? What is wrong about our skin and our features, other than some conqueror deeming them inferior?) Sexual experience, anger, service, and single motherhood are not necessarily bad. It's sexism that shapes our understanding of these traits. The real trouble is that Black women are reduced to *only* these things. And the caricatures of Jezebel, Mammy, Sapphire, and the Matriarch are reinforced—often by our loved ones, as the profiles in this chapter illustrate—from the time we are little Black girls.

While Black communities, for the most part, insist they do not believe Black women are congenitally sex hungry or bestial or subservient or unattractive, they also often insist Black women *prove* we are not who White folks say we are. Our loved ones too often feed the distortions by asking us to live our lives in deference to them. And the dirty secret is that many of our families and friends and communities benefit from the fact that Black women remain yoked to old stereotypes.

I focus here on how our Black communities reinforce distorted views of Black women and girls because hearing lies about us from people we know and love can be most damaging. Any Black woman who has been awake to the state of race and gender in this country expects to hear lies about us in the majority culture. We hate it. We know the damaging effect it has on people's perceptions of us. We call it out. Most of us know to question portrayals of Black women in media, academia, government, and other institutions. We are hip to the game.

But we trust the people who love us to tell us the truth. We expect them to have our best interests at heart. When, for instance, we hear reductive ideas about womanhood and sexuality from our parent and pastor, it may be easier to be ashamed of ourselves than to question them.

Kristina*

To exist in the Black church, a woman should be feminine, pure, and submissive to men. I learned that growing up. The pastor's wife, or First Lady, is the example for women in

---

* The profiles throughout Part II are the result of hourlong (sometimes longer) interviews that have been condensed and distilled to capture each interviewee's story and voice. All women were given the opportunity to review their profiles before publication. Pseudonyms have been used when requested.

the congregation to follow. My father was an evangelist. My mother, with her light skin and hazel eyes and meticulous makeup and jewelry, was the First Lady.

My dad traveled a lot to other churches. I can remember being in the car with my father and my mother and my brother doing road trips to these rural White conservative spaces. Sometimes my father would bring me up on stage. "Here's my daughter. She's taken this vow of purity." People would come up to me after church and give me money. They'd say, "Keep going, young lady." It's so weird to say that out loud now, but at the time it was very normal. Some girls were offered thousands of dollars to remain virgins until after high school graduation.

My father believes in male church leadership. He used to say things like, "I cannot sit under a woman pastor. I can't sit under a woman who is trying to tell me how to be a man." I sat in several church services where it was no problem for a man to tell me what I, as a young woman, should desire and aspire to be, though. And all those things were patriarchal in nature, like how to keep and attract a man. What if you don't even like men? Nobody ever said.

I think I understand why I was so quiet when I was younger. I decided not to talk because the questions I had were probably not going to be answered in the way that I needed them to be. It was easier to be quiet. I didn't have the language or the safety to know that it would be okay for me to go to my parents and say, "Hey, I think I like girls."

I sat in hundreds of church services and was taught that I should wait to have sex with my husband [who would then lead my family]. I just knew that anything different was not okay. I married a man in my late twenties and had a baby before I realized I was gay.

I'm thirty-four now. I'm married to a woman, and the freedom I feel with my wife is contrary to everything my parents still believe. But I'm still working through religious trauma and internalized homophobia that make it a struggle to live outwardly and freely.

Some of our loved ones believe the common narratives about Black women and girls. Some of them simply know the world we live in. I have spoken to many Black mothers who are hard on their daughters because they know the world will be hard on them. Grandmama may not believe that Black girls are loud and prone to being "fast," but she knows that our broader society does, and so she strictly enforces rules of female comportment because she wants her girl to succeed, to be accepted. But in the shorthand of everyday life, intentions get lost. Whether well-meaning or malicious, policing feels like a refutation of our alrightness.

Carolyn

Mama was really my great-great-grandmother's sister. When I was born, she looked at my biological mother and thought, "She can't raise this baby. This baby live over here now." My mother died when I was six and the arrangement became permanent.

Mama was born in 1909 and she was both ahead of her time and a product of her time. She got divorced in the 1930s when folks didn't do that. She worked several jobs to care for her children rather than deal with her husband's shit. She was one of the first women in the nation to get a barber's license. She worked for a company that didn't promote women or Black folks, but they promoted *her*. She was a trailblazer.

Mama told me—a little Black girl, growing up in the 1990s—that I could be anything I wanted to be. And she made sure that was true. When my teacher kept favoring this little light-skinned girl with a swinging ponytail over me, Mama marched up to that school and snapped on everybody for not giving me the same opportunities that they were giving this other child. She fought for me.

Mama was also the person who helped teach me that dark skin was bad and that I—a dark-skinned, fat girl with short hair—was not beautiful. She didn't *say* that. But I got the message. I noticed the way she vigilantly watched my skin in the summertime, calling me in before I could get any darker. And I remember when I wanted to wear a black dress to the prom, she said "no," because folks wouldn't be able to see me. There were plenty of other comments here and there. I knew the deal.

I graduated from one of the most prestigious universities in the country. I have two master's degrees. I have a doctorate. And I think my Mama still might have believed my greatest accomplishment was giving birth to two non-dark-skinned babies. She was alive to meet my oldest. And if you look at [my daughter's] baby pictures, she is always wearing some big head covering. That's because my mama was trying to "help" another generation and protect the baby's "pretty yellow skin."

Mama wasn't being malicious. She wanted the best for me. I know that our society does not value Blackness or dark skin or fatness. America believes women should be beautiful, and it doesn't find any of these things beautiful. Mama wasn't against a woman using her feminine wiles to get ahead, but she was pretty sure that wasn't available to the likes of me. I think she thought, *Let's try and fight for you in other ways. I need you to be the smartest person in the room because you'll never be the prettiest.*

But here's the thing. As a dark-skinned woman, I don't need to be prepared for colorism. I live it. I struggle to feel beautiful in my skin. Still. Even now, when everybody is allegedly all about inclusion and body positivity. I often feel that I should be grateful just to be included in spaces, since no one is checking for dark-skinned people and Black women, anyway. This idea of me as automatically less than affects everything I do. Mama thought she was helping, but she made me feel like maybe she believed what society thought about me—that maybe they were right.

* * * * *

They are not right. Nor are our loved ones who traffic in harmful stereotypes to steel our spines against a harsh world. The strong Black woman stereotype is insidious in part because it feels like a compliment and it is rooted in small truth. Black women do often have to endure disproportionate difficulty in life, most of it the result of systemic racism and patriarchy. Hard times can build resilience. But just because we have had to bear unthinkable pain without complaint doesn't mean we *should*.

Lucy

I have dealt with significant depression since I was a teenager. My parents were very against my seeing a therapist. They thought I should just be stronger. My father said I didn't need to talk to "some White lady," I just needed to pray.

Part of it was this whole stupid strong Black woman notion. Whatever negative feelings or whatever depression we may have, we are expected to put on a strong face and take it. Our mothers did and our grandmothers did and our great-grandmothers did. And their lives were much harder than ours.

It wasn't until I had a suicide attempt and ended up in the ER that I was finally able to see a therapist on a regular basis. She prescribed medication for me, but I didn't take it faithfully. I was still living with my parents at the time and they were against it—even after I spent five days in the hospital following my suicide attempt.

It was hard for me to shake the idea that I should just be able to manage. Even when I was in grad school and a thousand miles away from my parents, I only went to see a therapist when I was in absolute crisis. And when she prescribed medication, I still heard my family in my head. It's only in the last two or three years that I have taken medication and seen a therapist regularly.

The older I get, the more I realize how many Black people are self-medicating. My dad has severe PTSD from his time in the military. He self-medicates with alcohol. I see other family members self-medicating with alcohol or drugs or food, too. These people will never, ever go to a therapist or take medication or anything like that, because they think that if they succeed in their career or try harder or pray harder, everything will be fine.

You know, I think some of our great-grandmothers and great-great-grandmothers might look at us and say, "You got to be kidding me! I would have loved to be able to see a doctor or talk to someone about things that I went through. You have all these things at your disposal; don't use me as your crutch or a rationale for your stupidity."

* * * * *

This unceasing barrage of warped narrative and the tacit acceptance of even those who claim to love us is hypnotizing. Each encounter and endorsement of distortion is like a magician's swinging pendulum, deepening a trance.

Daddy obsesses over your sexual purity and sneers at women as leaders.

Swing . . . swing.

The boss suggests that your attitude is intimidating . . . aggressive . . . no offense.

Swing . . . swing.

Sister tells you to toughen up and ignore your depression; strong Black women don't do therapy and meds.

Swing . . . swing . . .

Six o'clock news says a Black woman was killed by police and no one is marching or asking questions.

Swing . . . swing . . .

Grandmama says, "Come in out the sun now. You already dark enough."

Swing . . . swing.

Sister, this is how we become bewitched and learn to feel shame about parts of ourselves that are benign—singleness . . . fatness . . . vulnerability . . . loudness—qualities that veer too close to stereotypes.

We become estranged from our instincts and desires and who we would want to be if we were not trying to outrun racist and sexist distortions or leaning into somebody else's view of respectable Black womanhood. We devote ourselves to careers and relationships and situations that we do not want. We work ourselves to the point of breaking in service of other people's needs. We ignore our own sexual pleasure or, sometimes, feel compelled to perform sexiness for the male gaze. We hate our natural hair unless it "behaves." We swallow our righteous anger. We fall prey to misogynist charlatans who promise to "fix" us and make us more "high value" as partners. We hate other Black women who do not conform and devote their lives to disproving untruths. And we teach younger generations of Black women to do the same. We become untethered from our humanity, our divine nature, and each other.

The distorted image of Black womanhood is killing us— our bodies, our spirits, our possibilities. To fully embrace our Black woman selves and be free—to see ourselves and our sisters clearly—we must first learn to spot the distortions that obscure our true natures. We must separate lies from veracity like wheat from chaff.

I realized this while reckoning with my identity as a yogi. Yoga, an ancient communal practice of spirituality created by Brown people in the Global South, has come to be associated in the West with thinness, Whiteness, youth, athleticism, and exclusivity—expensive studios, retreats, and workout wear. Not middle-aged Black women in large bodies. Not me. I was not aware of all the Black women, through time, who have been devoted to yoga practice, including Mother Rosa Parks. There is a delightful photo of the civil rights activist, age sixty, doing yoga. She has the same sweet face with wire-framed glasses we've come to know from history books, but she is clad in a black leotard and tights.

I had to clearly recognize the biases of Western yoga in order to embrace myself as a practitioner—even a teacher of yoga—with fat thighs and middle-age joints. I had to see the thin, young influencers in impossible poses; the pop-up ads for expensive and unnecessary equipment; and the ambivalent teachers in studios with few Black or Brown yogis on the wall (and even fewer in classes) as what they were: distortions of who has a right to what is, in reality, an individual and communal healing practice.

There is a word in Sanskrit, the language of yoga: *sat*. It means "true essence" or "true nature." *Sat* is also sometimes defined as "that which has no distortion." The concept of satya or "telling the truth" is a foundational pillar of yogic philosophy. It is one of the ethical restraints that are said to lead to enlightenment. The practice of *satya* means you must be clear, honest, genuine, and truthful in your relationships with others and yourself.

Black women are bombarded, from cradle to grave, with distortions beyond the metaphysical. We are fed a steady diet of Mammy, Jezebel, Sapphire, and the Matriarch. And so is everyone around us. Society—and too often even our closest friends and family—demands that we use our every action and deed to disprove this racist and sexist narrative. Our true natures become tangled in lies. We are rarely allowed to follow our instincts and desires. We are forced to spend too much time reacting and too little living free. We are robbed of choice. That is oppression.

You, my sister, deserve the freedom to discover and live out your truths. You deserve to revel in your true self, whoever she is. Do you know her? You cannot know who you really are unless you can untangle your true nature (and those of your sisters) from racist and sexist distortion. You first must be able to spot and interrogate the distorted stories of Jezebel, Sapphire, Mammy, and the Matriarch where they hide—everywhere, from the evening news to office codes of professionalism to your favorite Black celebrity forum or advice from your mama.

If we are to unbury our authentic selves and live free of oppressive narratives, we need to be experts at identifying and processing anti-Black woman propaganda wherever it appears—be it subtle or overt, conscious or unconscious.

ASK THIS
Unfair Portrayal or Not?

Good questions to ask, when confronted with a portrayal of Black women and girls:

- Does this presume that we are alright or deficient?

- Does the portrayal just happen to align with antebellum-era beliefs about African-descended women?

- What assumptions are being made?

- Would the judgment you are hearing make sense to anyone if said about someone who is not a Black femme? ("Justin, you better think twice about getting that PhD and buying that condo. No woman wants a man that independent. What will she be able to contribute?")

- Who is being uplifted? Who is being denigrated?

- How does it make you feel?

DO THIS
Learn to Spot and Interrogate the Distorted Stories Black Women Are Told about Ourselves

For the next week, write in your journal each day about your encounters with core stereotypes of Black women. (See "How to

Spot" at the end of this chapter for a cheat sheet on identifying these caricatures.) Write down the little things. The tossed-off proclamations from colleagues: "You're so intimidating!" The old (or new) school song lyrics. Write down the things that seem to be positive. The loud and sassy sidekick on your favorite show. The shared assertion in your sister-friend text thread that Black women instinctively know how to do anything and handle everything. Even note the times you catch *yourself* repeating stereotypes.

Spend some time interrogating these experiences:

- What stereotype did you encounter?

- Who or what was reinforcing the stereotype?

- How did the experience make you feel?

- If the experience was positive (say, an endorsement of Black women's resilience), how might you separate what is good from the reductive stereotype?

- Did you see any part of yourself in the stereotype?

- If there were people around you, what was their reaction to the stereotype?

- Where did you encounter stereotypes of Black women the most?

DO THIS
Meditate on a Mantra

A mantra is a sacred word or phrase repeated again and again to penetrate your unconscious and create a specific frame of mind. There is a mantra commonly used in yoga: *sat nam*. You know that *sat* means truth. *Nam* means name. Together? "True name" or "I am truth." In *Yoga Journal*, Karena Virginia says *sat nam* "is about expressing your true identity, not only for the benefit of yourself but also for others. No one else can express the exact combination of frequencies that you do. You are connected to all there is—the vast universal truth. In an infinite universe, you are unique. For the universe to be complete, your vibration is needed."

This week, spend at least five minutes each day meditating on the mantra *sat nam*. Take this time to focus your mind on your true self, apart from distorted and negative images of Black womanhood.

To do this, find a space to sit without distractions. Sit comfortably on the floor, on a meditation cushion, or on a chair. Set a timer. Straighten your back and let your hands rest in your lap, palms up or down. Breathe. As you exhale, release all the tension in your muscles. Do a scan of your body, from head to toe, to see where you may be holding stress.

Begin to chant your mantra, out loud or silently to yourself. Find a natural rhythm with your breath. Your mind may wander. Many people think the point of meditation is to stop the mind from thinking.

Sat nam

Explore in your journal who you would be if you were not trying to escape or lean into other people's visions of you, positive or negative.

HOW TO SPOT
Stereotypes of Black Women

Sapphire: Black woman as bestial

Sapphire is:

• Mad

• Aggressive

• Loud

• Masculine/emasculating

• Physically stronger than other women

A Sapphire by any other name: angry Black woman, Black bitch, hood rat

Jezebel: Black woman as oversexed

Jezebel is:

• Promiscuous

• Sexually aggressive

• Built for heterosexual sex (her body is an invitation to men)

• Always sexually available, unrapeable

A Jezebel by any other name: THOT, ho, fast-tail girl

Mammy: Black woman as perpetual servant

Mammy is:

• Without needs or desires of her own/self-sacrificing

- Tireless, resilient
- Maternal (but not for her own family)
- Undesirable by White cultural standards (fat, dark-skinned, broad-featured, nappy-haired)

A Mammy by any other name: Auntie

The Matriarch: Black woman as irresponsible single mother

The Matriarch is:

- Emasculating, dominating (chases away her men)
- Sexually irresponsible (too many babies she cannot support)
- Tireless, resilient, strong

The Matriarch by any other name: baby mama, welfare queen

CHAPTER 5

Know Your Truth

Freeing yourself was one thing,
claiming ownership of that
freed self was another.

—TONI MORRISON

Once you are aware of the distorted images of Black women and girls and how these images are fed to us, then begins the long process of finding out who you are without them—when you are not working to conform to what people say you should be or working to disprove who they say you are.

Excavating your authentic self is an art. Approach the work like an artist. Michelangelo is reported to have said, "The sculpture is already complete within the marble block before I start my work. It is already there, I just have to chisel away the superfluous material." You are already alright; you simply need to chisel away the admonitions and the warnings and the shoulds to make that plain.

We can find ourselves living to conform to what other people want from us, thinking it is the easier path. In truth, it is a path that makes us small and miserable.

Brandee Jasmine

I am a pastor in the African Methodist Episcopal church. I am Black. I am queer. I am outspoken. I am loud with my activism for Black folks, for women, for queer kids, for other marginalized people. I cuss sometimes. I love makeup and tattoos and dyeing my hair bright colors or just shaving it off. When I am most myself, I am purple, my favorite color. When I am purple, I am too much for a lot of folks. When I am purple, I am too much for the church.

People have said, "Her character is not appropriate for ministry." I've been told to be quiet. Compliant. I've gotten in trouble for cussing on Facebook about White supremacy in the Black church, not wearing the right clothes, and performing same-sex marriages. One of my dearest friends—another Black woman—distanced herself from me in order to gain a position of power in the church. She told me, "You stand out. . . . It scares the shit out of people. It scares the hell out of *me*. [You are who you are], but I can't be who I am."

They would be fine if I was quietly queer, quietly tatted, quietly purple. But, "She won't shut up. She won't sit down."

I tried. I stopped wearing corsets. I stopped wearing makeup. I shut up. I fit in. The people whom I loved in the church, whom I desperately wanted to love me, appreciated it. They would talk to me. I wasn't too much for them. I shrank so far. But I was miserable. I was miserable. I cannot live like that.

I've been in ministry for twenty-three years, fighting to do what God said to, to be who God said to be. Every so often, some twenty-year-old who's been AME all their lives will find me on Facebook or Instagram and ask me if God still loves them because they're queer. They'll find me and say they believe that they have a call to ministry. And they're afraid because they don't know how to be who God created them to be in a church where everybody is trying to create them in their own image. Everybody wants to re-create other people in their own image because that's how we see ourselves as powerful; that's too often how we understand our relationship with God. These young people just need somebody's permission to be who they are. That's why I have tried to stay in the church and fight. It is why I stay purple.

Now I have stretched and filled up my entire life. I do not feel the need to be small enough to fit into spaces that could have never held me in the first place. I don't give two flying fucks whether I fit in or not. I don't care whether I fit into the AME Church's concept of ministry. I do love the AME Church, but not more than I love myself. I especially love the queer kids and grown folk who are trying to figure out what it means to be made in the image of God and queer and AME. I love them, too, but not more than myself.

I don't know what happens next. I almost left the church last year. But, recently, I put on a corset and a pair of jeans and a blazer that I bought for General Conference. And I did my face and I had a photo shoot. It was transformative to be me again—the real, unapologetic me. I looked at myself and was like, "Oh, shit. There she is." I felt joy. I felt purple.

* * * * *

Sister, to know your truth you must become a student of yourself.

Yoga Sutra 2.4 says "Study thy self, discover the divine." The sutra describes a principle that has been important to my freedom journey: *Svadhyaya*, "one's own reading," the practice of self-study and the study of important texts. We can apply this to our freedom journey.

"The more we realize what we are not, the closer we come to realizing who or what we truly are," says Emma Newlyn, a yoga teacher and holistic therapist. "By studying 'the self' and recognizing our habits and thought processes, we realize how much of what we do and think is far from who we really know we are.

"When we listen to the ego, we often do things that don't always align with our true beliefs or intuition. The 'I' or small 'self' is mostly concerned with survival, which usually entails getting what it wants in all situations, and proving it is indeed 'the best' despite what consequences that might have for us. The small self judges, criticizes, fears, conditions, doubts. . . . By paying attention to, or 'studying' our 'self', we become more aware of the things we do that harm us, and also those that serve us and bring us closer to that process of 'yoking' or 'uniting' with the true Self."

To know your truth, you must become a people watcher, though the "people" you are watching is you. Newlyn advises observing yourself as though you were watching someone else. When are you your most expansive? When do you feel bound to code-switch? When are you silent? When do you stand tall, and when do you shrink? When are you happiest? What inspires you?

Of course, it is especially important to interrogate issues related to stereotypes of Black women and girls. For instance, have you been stifling your natural inclination to speak out at work over fear of being labeled angry or aggressive? Do you approach disagreements aggressively because that is what you learned it means to handle things like a Black woman? Do you feel guilt when you have to say no to what someone else wants of you?

Through self-reflection, we can find space between the stereotypes other people assign to us and who we truly are. We can create boundaries between false narratives for our own good. And we can see better where we have leaned into expectations of Black women to our own detriment.

Terri

Jezebel hasn't been my journey as a Black woman. People just don't see me like that. But the other stereotypes? Yes, I've gotten those.

I'm a professor at a predominately White institution, and some students relate to me like a Mammy figure. White kids come from these homogenous communities and aren't used to interacting with Black women in positions of authority. They expect this extraordinary level of support and nurture. I also get it from Black students, but that's different. Black students are usually feeling isolated on a majority White campus far from their families. But I have to draw a boundary there, too, for my own health and well-being.

I raised my children as a single mother from when they were pretty young. You know society carries all these negative ideas about single Black mothers. They think we're all on welfare and people approach us as if they are our saviors. I actually *did* need some support as a single mom. I was vulnerable when my children were very young, but I had a lot of assistance from my family and the kids' father. That's another thing: people think the men Black women have children with are never around, that they're in prison or just neglectful. That was not my situation, but I still had to navigate around that expectation.

Now, Sapphire: I feel like I have co-opted the angry Black woman stereotype in a way. Black women should be able to freely express their displeasure. If you've disrespected me, I am going to address it. Sometimes I *should* be angry. That's also part of being liberated and free. And it's part of being healthy. I try to contain all of that and it's gonna affect my body and my emotions. I need to be able to say, "You've made me mad." I can be angry if I want to, but I'll tell you when I'm mad. Don't assume that you know my emotions and feelings.

I am learning to use my anger more strategically. My father has this thing he says, "You could be dead right and dead wrong. You can be dead both ways." I was an appointed Board trustee and faced with an issue around race and justice that was important to me. I wanted other people to see what I was seeing. The way I thought I could do that was to be antagonistic. And I misfired. I wasn't renewed for another term. I should have played a little bit better with others, I guess. That's hard for me to say because I think if you have integrity, you speak out. But I lost the opportunity to make the change I wanted to make.

I feel free from those stereotypes now—the Mammy, Matriarch, and Sapphire. I didn't always. It's been a journey. I became a full professor around the time George Floyd died. In that moment I realized that I needed to present myself as a model of how to walk through this world as a Black person. If you want liberated children, you have to model that. What use is my education and my voice if I'm not gonna use it to address what is happening with my own people, if I'm not going to use it for our betterment? My mother just passed and so I am thinking about legacy. What I have done and will do for my people has become more critical than the labels other people want to place on my Black womanhood.

* * * * *

While you are working to uncover your authentic self, it may be necessary to create boundaries against the well-meaning advice of others who believe they know what is best for you. People are not used to free Black womanhood. They are not used to believing Black women should live outside of American society's and the Black communities' strictures. People who love you want you to be safe, successful, and accepted. They may not understand the costs you are willing to pay for your liberation. (More on that later.)

A critical skill that we must learn, sister, is how to reject what other people want of us when we discover it is not what is good for us. Mammy mythology says Black women and girls exist for the needs of others and have no personal desires. It is a myth that dies hard. You have agency. Part of knowing your truth is learning how to use it, including finding a way to erase old tapes and conditioning about how you should live.

Angela

I was walking on campus at Miami University in Oxford, Ohio, when I got a phone call from my *tio* in the Dominican Republic. Now this man has never rang my line for a single thing ever. So I'm thinking there's some emergency that is happening in the Motherland because why else would he be calling me? After some small talk, my uncle said, "I heard you decided to go natural. Just don't take it too far."

Some people in the DR love all the racial and ethnic diversity that makes our island beautiful and at the same time idolize everything proximate to Whiteness. I grew up hearing that if my elbows were dark they needed to be lightened with Ambi, and that my hair at age seven was too much and needed to be relaxed. The straighter and the longer my hair was, the better. I heard these things so often in my upbringing that it doesn't even matter if my family is with me, I hear those messages playing.

I've chosen to turn off the volume and strip the messages I learned from my family of their power. I have to in order to celebrate my Black hair.

It helped in college when I found Nadia, a sister who was doing hair in her dorm room. She had products and a real hood dryer and everything. She saved me when I got my hair tangled up in some Bantu knots. She gently detangled my natural hair, washed it, conditioned it, flat-twisted it. I had the freshest twist out, man. She gave me tools to figure out how to navigate my natural hair. She *cared for* my natural hair like it was beautiful, because it was.

I experienced this shift. I saw me wearing my natural hair and I was like, "This is me. This is who I actually am." I had never felt that way with straightened hair. You should see me when I have my Amara La Negra afro. Just big and voluminous. If it's cold, the 'fro could be earmuffs; if it's hot, it could be sunglasses. Just glorious! I love the way my natural hair feels and the way it looks. It compliments my outfits. I became really expressive with my clothing after I went natural because I was like, "Oh, if this hair's going to be fabulous, I got to have clothes that fit the vibe." My other stuff wasn't hitting anymore. There was a freedom that came from just being able to recognize and show off the real me.

Those messages about what equals acceptable Black hair are not easy to ignore completely, though. As a matter of fact, just a few months ago I got my hair done. Tried something new. I showed the hairdresser this style on Pinterest—several braids blending together into one long braid. When she was done and whipped me around in front of the mirror, I thought, *Yo! Sis, that braid is really long!* The braid was tickling mid-back and I had to go to work the next day. I ended up pulling a sister at work aside and asking, "Keep it a buck, now. Is this

braid giving too long? Is it giving ghetto? 'Cause I'm worried."
You know, now that you ask, I don't exactly know what the
line is between a respectable braid and one that isn't. . . .

I try to do my part by affirming little Black girls' hair. I'm
really intentional when I see Black girl hair. I'm like, "Queen!
Your hair looks so cute! That bow is *it*!" Now these stores have
all these cute things for Black girls. If you're a Black girl and
I know you, you're about to get a greeting card, a coloring
book—something that loves on you real good and reflects you.
I'm just really conscious about the way that I talk about their
expression of self because I don't want to do to them what was
done to me.

* * * * *

In yoga, *svadhyaya* includes not just self-study, but the study
of sacred texts. Black women have sacred texts. Take the lit-
erary classic *Their Eyes Were Watching God*, by Zora Neale
Hurston. It is the story of Janie Crawford, a forty-something
woman returning to her hometown after an absence. She
recounts to her friend Phoeby where she has been, weaving
a tale of oppressive marriages, abuse, love, racism, triumph,
and, ultimately, Janie's freedom. You will not read Hurston's
story and remain unchanged. Hurston is among our Black
femme sages.

Toni Morrison. Alice Walker. bell hooks. Audre Lorde.
Zora Neale Hurston. Ntozake Shange. Jamaica Kincaid. Pearl
Cleage. Roxane Gay. Deesha Philyaw. Chimamanda Ngozi
Adichie. Their work renders Black women fully, in all our
humanity and complication. You must study this work, sister.

These women create mirrors that reflect our experiences. They write freedom stories. Read them.

DO THIS
Write Your Life

Imagine what free Black womanhood looks like for you. Write the life you want. Don't worry about where you are today. Where would you be if you alone were in charge of the script? Assess your goals. Are you working to put down roots when you are really a nomad? Are you wearing your hair a way your mom likes or your man likes, but you hate? Have you endured a way or place of worship that does little to feed your soul? Explore what your authentic life could be.

DO THIS
Meditate

Are you keeping up your freedom rituals? Don't forget this important foundation for your liberation, especially meditation. Sitting silently is a wonderful way to listen within and gain clarity about your true self. You needn't force it. Just sit, breathe, and watch your thoughts as they come and go. I've had many epiphanies and untangled several challenges simply sitting on my meditation cushion. Make sure that you are making daily space for reflection, even if just five or ten minutes.

CHAPTER 6

Celebrate the Real You

Deal with yourself as an individual
worthy of respect and make everyone
else deal with you the same way.

—NIKKI GIOVANNI

It is one thing to unearth the woman you are; it is another to love that woman. If Black women are to be free, we must learn to greet our real selves with friendliness, compassion, delight, and equanimity. In yoga, these qualities are called *brahmaviharas*, or "four immeasurables." They offer a framework for cultivating positive behaviors and minimizing negative ones. They represent a way to cultivate love and goodwill. Sister, you must cultivate love and goodwill toward your authentic self. This is true even, and perhaps especially, when your identities and experiences resemble some negative stereotypes about Black women.

You may have endured difficult things. You may have made grievous mistakes. Both of these things are part of the human condition, but society does not offer Black women and girls much grace. You have to offer yourself grace. As social justice activist Bryan Stevenson writes in *Just Mercy*, "Each of us is more than the worst thing we've ever done." You are not your trauma or your fuck-ups, but they are a part of the whole you. And that whole deserves celebration.

Nikki

I used to think there were parts of myself that I needed to eliminate to be acceptable. I have come to learn that the opposite is true. Freedom happens by inclusion rather than exclusion. Freedom is accepting the beauty in your whole self.

When I introduce myself I introduce all of my parts: I'm Nikki. I'm a recovering addict. I'm a recovering alcoholic. I'm a survivor of childhood and adult sexual trauma. I'm a mother. I'm a yoga therapist. I'm a teacher. I'm a grandmother. I'm a great-grandmother. I'm a bitch. I'm a former sex worker. All of those identities have been on Team Nikki. How dare I think about excluding them? How dare I make them bad? They've all been part of my survival. Healing and moving toward more freedom and liberation, for me, has come from including and honoring all of those parts. All of them. They are part of my whole.

We are a culture that depends on external validation. All our lives we get this external programming dumped on us, and it changes who we think we are and what we should be. Years and years ago, for instance, I was going through a divorce. It was so hard. But I came to realize that the pain I was feeling was not because I thought my husband and I should stay together, but because I was very attached to a vision of who I should be. I needed to be a wife. We become attached to these ideas and images of what our existence *should* look like.

But the wholeness is still there. One of my teachers, Gary Craft, says, "Examining our conditioning is our ticket to freedom." Strip away the external conditioning and you find wholeness. We have to have an unshakeable personal belief that we are complete.

We learn to celebrate our whole selves by pausing and consciously withdrawing from doing to focus on reconnecting with self. Our culture programs us to do, do, do. And we lose track of our personal understanding of what it means to be right.

We learn to celebrate our whole selves in community. There is a little tribe of women in my life. I give these women spiritual consent. They give me spiritual consent. It's a trusted, rooted relationship. They call me in. They call me back to true myself.

We learn to celebrate our whole selves by seeing the completeness in younger generations. Little Black girls. Babies. You know, when we are born there is no Black or White, no boy or girl, no concepts like that. There is nothing to seek or look for or run after. It's all already there. We are simply divine. There is a picture of me holding one of my great-granddaughters when she was just two hours old. I show it all the time when I am teaching. It is a touchstone. I am looking at my newest descendant and I am thinking, *This is wholeness.*

* * * * *

The lie is that Black women and girls are often reduced to *only* negative traits. That does not mean there are not those of us for whom these descriptions are true. For instance, some Black women and girls unskillfully communicate through anger. This is not some innate quality of their Black femmeness. (Angry folks abound. Have you watched the news?) Often aggression is the last resort of someone who is unsupported and has few coping skills.

If you recognize negative traits in yourself, it is your obligation to resolve them, but know that your flaws are not an "I told you so." They don't prove anything about Black women or girls. They don't let systemic racism and sexism off the hook. And they don't make your full self unworthy or valueless.

Even when we don't make mistakes, misogynoir has a way of rendering as flaws even benign traits that depart from Whiteness, middle-classness, straightness, and maleness. Sister, there is nothing wrong with African American Vernacular English. There is nothing wrong with large bodies. There is nothing wrong with being an unmarried mother. There is nothing wrong with righteous anger. There is nothing wrong with independence. It is just that these traits are often twisted when they are attached to a Black femme.

Mistakes, trauma, or benign traits—they are a part of your divine whole that deserves honor.

Renee

I went to a predominantly White private school for most of my adolescent life. My mother believed I would get a better education going to school with White people. She wasn't wrong for that, but I think she didn't consider what it feels like for a Black girl in a place like that—where no one would let me forget that I was different and that the ways I was different were not okay.

I was plus-size shopping at Lane Bryant before they had fashionable clothes . . . when it was just the flower patterns. Went to Favor or Payless for my wide-width shoes. I was the biggest one in the class, dressing like a teacher. My hair was different. I talked with a lisp. My classmates would come back from break talking about trips to Paris and Monaco; I spent my vacations playing with my friends on the block. White kids wanted to know, "Is your family poor?"

I started feeling this constant anxiety, like I was always holding my breath, waiting to be judged. The education I needed to reinforce loving myself wasn't in those private school walls. It was in the neighborhood with all the kids who looked like me and who never questioned that I was big and Black and my hair was kinky.

I had to learn to love the things about my Black woman self that made me "other" as a child. I am 340 pounds and five foot eight. There's no way in hell you aren't going to see me. And you should see me. I'm a dreamer. I believe the impossible is always possible. I believe that there is victory in speaking up and fighting for what's right. I color outside the lines.

Renee is a tangled web and I love on all of her. I bathe with peppermint soap every day. I grease my skin with coconut oil and cocoa butter. You know when you put that on your skin that little shine comes and does something to your little heart. I love that there's a vibration in the way I walk. I listen to binaural beats to sleep well at night and get some peace of mind. It's all love. I am committed to doing the things that feed me, because that is freedom—being able to do what you do without worrying about being ostracized because of it. Freedom is not waiting on joy. Like, I usually don't wear jumpsuits, because of my FUPA, you know? But yesterday I was like, "I'm putting the jumpsuit on."

I am forty-three years old. If I'm lucky, I have maybe thirty more years on this earth. I want my thirty years to be focused on something other than making sure that I'm showing up to fit someone else's comfort. Nobody has any authority to make me feel anything but how I allow them to make me feel. If you are uncomfortable with my full self, that's your problem. It's not mine.

* * * * *

Just as loving ourselves makes it easier to love our sisters, loving our sisters makes it easier to love our whole selves. This is the reality of our interdependence. To learn to celebrate yourself, practice looking upon other women and girls with loving, not critical, eyes. Especially girls. I have spoken to many mothers who learned to appreciate some physical trait or habit of their own only when they saw it reflected in their daughters. Intergenerational love is powerful and transformative.

Keesha

Many years ago, I decided to embrace the principles of Kwanzaa as a lifestyle. They are *umoja* (unity), *kujichagulia* (self-determination), *ujima* (collective work and respon-sibility), *ujamaa* (cooperative economics), *nia* (purpose), *kuumba* (creativity), and *imani* (faith). This is what helps me to show up in spaces confident in who I am and bold about showing my Blackness. I'm intentional.

When you look in the mirror and see a person that is beautiful, worthy, and deserving, then you start hearing the pearls of wisdom that ride on the waves of the universe. I learned to accept who I am and recognize that the things people want me to believe about my African ancestry are not true. The way you get there is by reading, talking, and con-necting with other people of your same experience. Then your sisters look different because you know them and feel connected.

I am dark-skinned. And when I was young, I went to a pre-dominately White all-girls school. That's where I learned that I am not just Black; I am *black*. White people tend to treat Black folks differently based on how much melanin we have. And we tend to assimilate aspects of that thinking. So I had always wished to be lighter, but never darker. Then I met this one little girl.

She was a pretty little girl with deep chocolate skin. I was curious about her confidence, having grown up believing that dark skin was a curse. She was such a bright light. But I did notice that she would do this one thing: she would hide her mouth with her hand when she would smile or laugh. I got her to take her hand down and I asked her why she always did that. She told me, "My teeth are crooked and I don't want people to laugh at me." I said, "Well, my teeth are crooked, too. How about this? We make a deal that we're just going to smile and that's okay."

That little girl grew up, became an entertainer, and started a dance company. She unexpectedly joined the ancestors this year. But that day, she and I, we helped each other feel more comfortable in our skin. That moment was part of my evolution to self-love and accepting myself as God made me.

* * * * *

Learning to celebrate your whole self—(perceived) warts and all—may be the hardest step on the pathway to liberation. It is hard but critical. Nothing works if we cannot do this. (Do not pass Go. Do not collect $200.) Remember, sister, you must believe you deserve to be free.

Celebrating yourself requires an ability for nuance, forgiveness, and grace. You have to believe in your inherent alrightness. There can be no ifs, ands, or buts. You cannot say, "I am a good woman *but* I am a single Black mom." Or, "I will celebrate myself *if* I lose 50 pounds." "I love this part of me *and* hate this other part." This is non-negotiable.

Love your authentic self. Celebrate your authentic self. Full stop.

DO THIS
Find an Avatar

Hopefully, you are detoxing from negative images of Black women. Allow me to suggest some nourishment to take the place of the things you have ditched. Find an avatar. An avatar is an icon or figure representing a particular person—in this case, you. For instance, I love yogi Jessamyn Stanley's work. I read her book *Yoke*. I follow her on social media. She is Black and plus-size and I see myself reflected in her. She helps me love the person who shows up on my mat and see what is possible for someone in a similar body. Mainstream media celebrates a very narrow subset of women. Go beyond that to honor other women like you.

DO THIS
Write a Love Letter to Yourself

In your journal, write a love letter to yourself. Be creative and specific, as if you were writing to a lover. Write about all the things you love about yourself and (now, here comes the hard part) try to write lovingly about some of the traits you struggle with. Write about how your FUPA keeps your hands warm in the winter or how your loud mouth has talked you into opportunities that other folks have missed. Once the letter is written, I invite you to add reading it to your daily ritual as a reminder that you are alright and loved by the most important person in your life.

CHAPTER 7

Understand the Cost of Liberation

Are you sure, sweetheart, that you want to be well? . . . Just so's you're sure, sweetheart, and ready to be healed, cause wholeness is no trifling matter. A lot of weight when you're well.

—TONI CADE BAMBARA

They ain't ready for you, sis.

You can't take your full self everywhere. Especially when you are a Black woman whose very existence has been historically derided and demeaned. The world is not ready for Black femme freedom. It does not want it and tries to kill it when it sees it. We can free our minds and perceptions from misogynoir, but our freed selves will still exist in a racist and sexist world. Free Black women will still enter spaces where our authentic selves are unwanted or unsafe. Other folks' ideas around Black womanhood will still stand in the way of things we need and desire. Until the great day the racist patriarchy is smashed, liberation for Black women will always come at a cost. And you, my sister, have to be good at balancing your ledger to determine when and how much you are willing and able to pay.

This is especially true in the American workplace. Black women have higher labor force participation rates than other women[1] but suffer a greater poverty rate than all other racial groups except for Native women.[2] We make 64 cents to a White man's dollar[3] and are disproportionately segregated into low-wage service- and care-industry jobs.[4] At the same time, more than 84 percent of us are primary, sole, or co-breadwinners for our households. It is as it ever was; Black women are grist for the capitalist mill and particularly vulnerable to capitalist ideas of power and professionalism that lean heavily on sexism, racism, and other biases.

Being a Black woman in the American workforce demands that we learn to make strategic compromises. The cost of bringing our authentic selves to the workplace is even steeper for sisters without the privilege of class or education. But all working Black women have to fight to exist authentically while protecting ourselves and our ability to support our families from the damage of people's biases.

Laura

I'm looking for a job in tech. They pay big. People are ashamed to talk about wanting money, but security is important to me.

My parents struggled. I grew up seeing the difficult options my mom had to choose between to make ends meet. And I now know what money affords. It gets me the autonomy to use my passport to travel places and experience different cultures. Money lets me live in a safe and supportive community. I want to have a family one day. I'm thirty-six. I don't have a partner. I may have to harvest my eggs, while I can still use them. I could have a high-risk pregnancy, especially as a Black woman, given our maternal health stats. I may have to pay for a surrogate. It's like $15,000 to get your eggs harvested and keep them frozen, and another, probably, $200,000 for the surrogacy process. Adoption is expensive, too. We live in a capitalist society. Yes, it's trash. But capitalism isn't going anywhere right now. In this country, money gets you a little bit of freedom.

I work in banking now. I know the cost of being a Black woman in corporate America, and I am willing to pay it. I code-switch at work. I sacrifice telling the raw and honest truth about the prejudice that happens in the workplace because responding to racism and sexism in the "wrong" way would make me a target—the one they're going to figure out how to push out. I don't have the luxury of frankness; I have to be manipulative. People get afraid of the word *manipulation*, but I've told my therapist that manipulation is a superpower. I use it to influence people, to get what I want, which is more Black and Brown and disabled and LGBTQIA people— especially Black women—winning around me. When that happens, maybe the cost of existing in a corporate space won't be so high for women like me.

There are parts of myself that I will not give up, though. I had a Zoom meeting with this career coach once—a Black woman I found on my university's Alumni Association site. Highly recommended by a friend. She recommended that if I want to work in anything other than diversity, equity, and inclusion [DEI], I need to get rid of my big, natural hair and photos of Black people behind me on the wall. She pointed out to me how she had positioned herself in a room with generic accent pieces. It took everything I had to keep my face calm. I got angry at first. But then, I thought to myself, that woman has had to sacrifice so much of her identity that she now thinks anything related to Blackness is either DEI-focused or potentially scary to White people. I understand how she may have gotten there, but I don't want to be that person.

* * * * *

There is no universal right or wrong to how you navigate the workplace. Your boundaries around what cost is too high to pay are personal and influenced by your values, needs, and desires, and your privileges and oppressions.

I will not tell you, in the name of freedom, to walk out of any job that dares to dictate what a Black woman's hair should look like. You may decide that the loss of a few favorite hairstyles is worth the ability to support your family or gain critical experience or, hell, buy a Louis bag (get money, girl!). You may decide to compromise a bit of your authentic self, for a time, so the sisters who come after you don't have to do the same. No judgment if your current job is not a cost you are willing to pay to be your full, free self. No judgment if you leave your cubicle for lunch and never come back. It is your decision. But I urge you to know the difference between compromising to get something you need or want and sacrificing your humanity. It is a perilously tight needle to thread.

Minda

I spent fifteen years in corporate America. For the first ten, I wasn't strategically compromising; I was sacrificing. This happens a lot with Black women. We do what we have to do to get ahead, to get in the room. It's strategic, but it isn't a compromise. Compromise means both parties are moving and trying to give and take. When Black women are involved, much of the time, everybody else is getting what they want and we're getting maybe just a pinch.

My full name is Yasminda, but that name always created some kind of angst in White people when they saw it. Minda made people feel comfortable. I gave up my name. I wore my hair the straightest. I bought clothes that helped me feel like I belonged, even if I didn't have money for them. I laughed at certain jokes at my expense and didn't speak up when I needed to. I made other people feel comfortable, even if it made me shrink.

I rose up the ladder. But at the expense of my own well-being. My mental and physical health deteriorated. I developed anxiety and panic attacks. The experience started to impede how I saw myself. I was no longer ambitious. I questioned every decision I made in the workplace. There were times when someone would say something demeaning to me and I would become so paralyzed that I couldn't get my words out.

Once I was in a team meeting with, maybe, fifteen other people. I was the only Black woman. One of my colleagues called me "the Black girl" in the meeting. Not Minda, but "the Black girl." Yeah. I left that meeting and cried in my car. I felt like I'd done everything that the dominant culture had said to do. Still, I wasn't getting treated with dignity and respect. I felt hopeless.

The verdict in the Trayvon Martin case was a pivotal moment. It made me ask myself who would stand up for me if I could not stand up for myself. I realized that I had more power than I was allowing myself. I decided to center myself in my work narrative. I looked for networks that could help me navigate a little bit better. I aligned with people who could speak up on my behalf when I wasn't able to. I took back my power and, eventually, I walked away from corporate America, because not only am I unwilling to sacrifice; I can no longer compromise.

Today I have a career using my voice to make sure that there are no more tears cried because of toxic workplaces for Black women. But my exit took time. And many of us can't leave. I have this concept of healing in the meantime. What Black women can do is ask ourselves: *How can I make this situation work for me?* Humanity, dignity, equity, and respect— those are the table stakes. I may not be able to leave my job, but I can demand to be called by my name. I can advocate for myself. Self-advocacy is self-love.

* * * * *

Physiological and safety requirements are at the root of psychologist Abraham Maslow's hierarchy of needs, the theory that mental well-being is predicated, in part, on fulfilling innate human needs in order of priority. We need things like food, shelter, clothing, and security most of all. That is why work, which affords Black women access to these important things, is a space that forces such hard decisions and compromises.

But work is not the only space where Black women must calculate the cost of being our authentic selves. Maslow says human beings need love, intimacy, and a sense of belonging, too. The rub, as I discussed back in chapter 2 is that Black women's parents and partners, our spiritual leaders, and our sisters—the people who love us—exist in this sexist and racist society with us. They also absorb those distortions of what is "wrong" with Black women and what we need to do to be good and acceptable.

This is how Black women became the fixers of the Black community. Black women's oppression has built our resilience, it is true. We are strong. But we are not unbreakable burden bearers and caretakers without our own needs. That idea, which has latched itself to the Black woman identity, is a perversion rooted in Sapphire and Mammy stereotypes. Black women raise the babies—and the grandbabies. Black women keep the church doors open, pay its bills, and serve the chicken at the repast. Black women march on the front lines: when Black men die, we are there. When our sisters die, we are often the *only* ones there. Black women bring home the bacon and fry it up in the pan. Black women comfort the community and hold it down. And we are often expected to do these things without respite or concern for our own health and well-being.

The community has learned to judge Black women who prioritize themselves. We learn to judge each other: "She knows she could just . . . [serve on this one committee; lead this one project; watch the babies this afternoon]!" But the cost of authenticity—prioritizing the need for a doctor's visit or rest or silence or creativity, or simply avoiding martyrdom—feels bigger than just disappointing our pastor, son, or sorority sister. When a Black woman prioritizes her authentic self and says no to overwork and perpetual service, it can feel like failing to live up to respectable strong Black womanhood. It is not a coincidence that Black women suffer high and disproportionate rates of lifestyle diseases—such as high blood pressure, diabetes, and heart disease—that could be mitigated through self-care, because rather than enforcing our boundaries and accepting this steep cost, many of us choose to sacrifice our own mental and physical health.

Sister, you must figure out the cost of disappointing your community from time to time, too. The math is difficult, I know. But living free means recognizing your inherent value and daring to prioritize your own health and well-being.

Black women are also forced to calculate the cost of liberation in romantic relationships. For the last decade, the conversation around Black women and heterosexual marriage—launched by the revelation in the 2010 United

States Census that we are half as likely to marry as our White counterparts—has been a campaign against Black femme authenticity. We are told *not* to trust our instincts, which, it is alleged, lean toward aggression (Sapphire), independence (the Matriarch), and promiscuity (Jezebel). We are asked to make ourselves smaller and subordinate, more "ladylike." Femininity is not our natural state, if the loudest voices are to be believed. Black women must be taught (usually by some man) how to be weaker, so our potential partners can feel strong. We are encouraged to "think like a man," so we can anticipate what male partners may want and the ways they may hurt us because they cannot be expected to curb their allegedly innate behavior.

There is far less discussion around how a Black woman might find a man (if, indeed, it is a man she wants) who suits her particular needs and personality. We are told that if we want to be loved, the cost is our authentic selves—our liberation. Many sisters resist, demanding partnership on their own terms. There is a cost for this, too.

Keturah

As a kid at Seventh Day Adventist school in New Orleans, I would hear other girls dreaming about their future selves with husbands and children, going to church on Sunday, and all that. But when I thought about my life, I was always with myself.

I am a child of divorce. My mom had five kids and I became sort of a de facto co-parent. This may be part of it. In reality,

I only did maybe 10 percent of what a full-time parent does. It was tiring. And I watched the way my mom sacrificed and my friends' moms sacrificed. I knew at a young age that I did not want children. And while I enjoy partnership, I'm indifferent to marriage. I prefer my autonomy and unconventional romantic relationships. I don't want to be constrained and I want control over my time and life.

I've made good use of my freedom. In forty-six years, I have become a New Yorker, traveled to twenty-seven countries, and lived and worked in four. I've taken financial risks that I would not have been able to take if I had a child or had to consult a partner. I've saved my money and invested it the way I want to. I've built deep and meaningful relationships. And I've had the time and solitude to understand myself. I am perfectly me, and that feels good.

But our society is structured around a certain life path. When you choose something different, like I have, you lose the benefits of conformity. There's about a hundred thousand laws on the books that benefit traditional marriage, especially financially. There is acceptance and respectability that you get from having children and a husband—especially Black women, who are always supposed to be nurturing somebody. There is an expected level of support that can come from having a partner or kids who are beholden to you.

I would love to be dating right now. I would love to have some testosterone energy in my life. But it's tricky. My marker for success is different. I am less likely to prioritize dating because I've never had the goal of heading to the altar followed by the maternity ward. I also learned early on that a lot of men want first right of refusal. They want the "carrot" of a ring to control the relationship. One time in my thirties, I went on a date with this dude. He told me it was "refreshing" that I wasn't "interviewing him for marriage like most women." I wasn't asking questions about how many kids he wanted or what he was looking for in a wife. He hinted that he was scared of a woman "trapping" him with a pregnancy. I told him I would not be having his children and that I was indifferent to his ring. He looked at me like he had seen a ghost: "Then why are you even *here*?!" There is an ease to dating when you are willing to play your "role" as a heterosexual woman. I don't have that ease, even with good dudes.

I'm beginning to think about these things as costs and I am becoming able to sort of own them. It doesn't seem like a big deal to me, though, because the things I would get if I conformed are not things I want.

My life feels like the right fit for me in a way that others don't always believe or understand. My primary partner is me, and there is no other person on this earth whose life I value more. I am 150 percent sure that any other choice would suffocate me and kill my soul. I am convinced that had I allowed myself to be talked into having some good man's child, staying in New Orleans, and going to church every Sabbath, I would be spiritually dead.

* * * * *

Loving yourself, sister, means doing no violence to your body, mind, or spirit—at work or anywhere else. The greatest of yoga's ethical principles is nonviolence, or *ahimsa* in

Sanskrit. *Ahimsa* calls for practitioners to cause no harm with thoughts, speech, and actions. I used to view this exhortation for peace as just a guideline for how to treat others. It is true that we shouldn't, say, commit violence against our children with thoughtless tongues that bruise their self-esteem. We shouldn't strike that belligerent and difficult coworker or neighbor, however good we imagine it might feel. We shouldn't even *think* it. I learned through yoga practice and studying *ahimsa* that both peace and love begin with me— with you, too, my sister. As we navigate the cost of liberation as Black women, we must commit not to do violence to ourselves.

At some time in your life, you will undoubtedly find yourself in a place where you cannot fully be your true Black woman self. That is a given. There are workplaces where a South Chicago drawl is deemed unprofessional. There are family elders with fixed ideas about who you should be. There are encounters with cops and other authority figures where out loud Black womanhood may put you in real mortal danger. Know this and be ready for it. There is no freedom from compromise; liberation comes from choosing where and how compromise happens. You will have to adapt. The challenge, sister, is to make your compromises with the understanding that it is not *you* who is unacceptable but the sexism and racism that require you to adapt.

It is critical to this process that you understand your personal needs and wants, as well as what it takes to access them. This will help you to calculate the price of staying in or disengaging from any situation. You may have grown up dreaming of a corner office and see wearing a corporate mask from 9 to 5 as a small price to pay. You may rely on the support and community of your church family and be willing to perform respectability and conservatism to maintain those relationships. You may have bills to pay and mouths to feed and need to appease the White patriarchy from time to time to make the rent. Don't we all?

One word about your needs and wants: it is smart to interrogate them. The same shoddy narratives that trouble us elsewhere influence the things we believe we need to live our best lives. Black women can wind up sacrificing bits of ourselves for jobs, partners, material things, and situations that do not align with our authentic identities. Do you really want a traditional heterosexual marriage, or are you running from the idea that Black women are perpetually single? Are you breaking your soul at a job you hate for the appearance of a lifestyle that doesn't really fulfill you? Every compromise isn't a good one.

The more privilege you have, the more choices and freedom you acquire. The answer to what you are willing to pay may change throughout your life as your understanding of self evolves, as your life and needs change, and as you grow more seasoned. It took me many decades to commit to being a Black woman with locs, tattooed forearms, and a penchant for public pronouncements on hot-button issues like race, gender, and sexuality—all choices of my personal expression that have costs in the world.

Believe this, sister, you cannot afford any compromise that kills your spirit or maims your well-being. Do not commit violence! Never compromise the love you have for your authentic self. Remember that you are divine. You are never to negotiate your own worth. What you must negotiate is how you move in an unfair system. Negotiate your boundaries, not your humanity.

Cost takes on a different meaning when you are paying or sacrificing for something you truly want. I can happily spend hundreds on books and gadgets. One of my besties will book a flight to a warm place with a beach faster than you can say "passport." Another loves a designer bag or shoe. We can afford these things and don't often miss what we spend on them, because they give us so much joy. But we all grumble when the electric bill comes due or the car needs repairs. I *want* new books—the feel of cracking the spine on a big, new hardback written by my favorite author . . . a stack of *five* new books, just sitting on my nightstand beckoning me on a literary journey. Ooh, it makes me giddy. (What can I say? I am a book nerd.) A new transmission for my car? Eh, not so much. However much the guy at the dealership tells me that will cost, it is invariably too damn high.

There will be costs you gladly pay to live freely, to have the authentic life that you want. Some choices may seem expensive to others, but for you no more significant than a handful of pennies.

It isn't fair. You need to know that, sister. It is not fair that sexism and Mammy mythology have fused the act of caretaking to Black womanhood, leaving little space for a sister who enjoys her own company. It is not fair that the idea of corporate "professionalism" is not wide enough to include a lovely uncommon name, hair with a bit of curl, and an affordable wardrobe. These biases are extra burdens that Black women do not deserve and should not have to carry.

You are not to "blame" for the ways you, as a Black woman, have to navigate the world. But you are responsible.

In his *New York Times* best-selling book *Inner Engineering: A Yogi's Guide to Joy*, yoga teacher Jagadish Vasadev, commonly known as Sadhguru, says that the word *responsible* has been misused. He points out that responsibility simply refers to our ability to respond.

He explains, "The quality of our lives is determined by our ability to respond to the varied complex situations that we encounter. If the ability to respond with intelligence, competence, and sensitivity is compromised by a compulsive or reactive approach, we are enslaved by the situation. It means we have allowed the nature of our life experience to be determined by our circumstances, not by us."

But all of our decisions, including the ones we make to live authentically, have costs. That is unavoidable. In this society that is so often unsafe and unwelcoming to your full, authentic, Black woman self, you must be responsible for balancing your own ledger sheet to the good. *Your good.* Own your power and take responsibility in situations that threaten your freedom.

DO THIS
Journal about the Costs You Are Paying

Where are the spaces in your life where you feel like you have to compromise your authentic self? Are you taking responsibility and navigating those places from a space of freedom? Are you sacrificing or strategically compromising? This week, spend time weighing these questions in your journal.

HOW TO SPOT
The Black Tax at Work

A 2020 study by Catalyst, shared by Black women's magazine *Essence*, found that our society imposes an additional "tax" on Black women (and men) who strive for success.[5]

- **Isolation:** The more financially and professionally successful Black women are, the fewer other Black people or women they will encounter.

- **Exclusion/pressure to conform:** A Black woman who is "the only" is often marginalized and faces extra pressure to conform to the majority culture in appearance and behavior. One woman in the *Essence* article spoke of scouring periodicals to be informed enough for office discussions; another learned golf to not be left out of a space where deals are closed.

- **Hypervigilance:** Fifty-four percent of 649 Black women and men surveyed who said they felt different because of their gender and race believed they had to be "on guard" when at work. These professionals were less likely to take professional risks or speak up in the workplace.

- **Poor health:** Black women often respond to workplace bias by leaning into the strong Black woman narrative, working extra hard to impress their managers. This can lead to overwork, anxiety, sleep deprivation, burnout, and overall poor health, as Black women neglect their own well-being.

CHAPTER 8

Practice Freedom

I have learned over the years that when one's mind is made up, this diminishes fear; knowing what must be done does away with fear.

—ROSA PARKS

You will get free, sister. You will not stay free. No one does. Life is not that way. Freedom is a practice. It is easy to practice when things are good. It is harder when you are overworked or overtired, lacking support, or facing a life-altering situation.

I wrote in chapter 3 about the crisis of liberation I experienced writing this book. Faced with my husband's illness, a demanding new job, and a big book project, I forgot that my well-being mattered beyond all the things I was hoping to accomplish and all my responsibilities.

Sister, when we are carrying a heavy load, the strong Black woman stereotype can be most punishing. When we are not being intentional, we return to type. We thoughtlessly act as if we can do everything and withstand anything for everybody. We unconsciously prioritize other people's deadlines, desires, wants, and needs over our own, because that is what Black women have been told we are supposed to do.

We give up on liberation. We forget that we are free to choose ourselves. And we forget that choosing ourselves actually leads to *better* outcomes than killing ourselves.

Bre

I think sometimes we Black femmes forget that what we want to make possible for others is for us, too. In 2020, I founded the Black Trans Fund (BTF), the first national fund dedicated to uplifting, resourcing, and building the capacity of Black trans social justice leaders. I've been operating these last three years as if Black trans communities deserve more joy and liberation than I do.

We are constantly evolving and growing, and part of choosing yourself again and again means periodic recommitment, reevaluation, and reconnection. That is what practicing liberation looks like. This year it became clear that it was time for me to do that work.

I felt the need for a radical reset in my body first. I had a kidney stone and was experiencing terrible pain. I burnt myself on a motorcycle. I fell and scratched my leg. Then everything felt like it was falling apart. Anything I touched in my home broke. I was unhappy with my work. It was like boom, boom, boom! Everything that could possibly go wrong did. I was starting to wonder why all this stuff was happening to me.

I think, for leaders, it is important for us to get clear about the things we need for survival. It is important that we build boundaries and step away for rest and recharge and then we come back and teach people what sustainable commitment looks like. If my fellow activists and I continue to do our work from a place of constantly giving, giving, and giving without taking care of ourselves, we are creating a new world of leaders who will repeat the same things. They will be overworked and underresourced and unable to build this new world that we're all talking about and investing in.

I am reimagining what the world would look like if I actually centered myself. Because *I* am Black trans joy. I want happiness and freedom for my community and for *me*. We all deserve that. And if I cannot embody joy and liberation—if I can't show folks how to walk and talk with their well-being centered—how successful can my work be?

I am focusing on joy, liberation, connection, and fun for myself.

I am being more transparent and vulnerable with the people around me. I admitted to a friend that I have an eating disorder, and we started talking about our eating disorders together. And that was amazing. I am connecting to people in a way that is radical for me.

I am journaling. I tell everybody: write that shit out! I will journal and then the next week I'll go back and I'll read my stuff. I'll highlight and take notes. Journaling lets me do inner work. It's intimate. It allows me space to say the things I need to say without judgment and then sit back with my feelings.

And I am having *fun*. Yes, I am! I have been building shit with LEGOs. I got an archery set and I'm out in the backyard shooting arrows. I go roller skating. When I'm on skates, it just feels like *everything*. It's the movement forward, the speed, the hair, the air blowing across your skin. There's a really good jam playing. You spin around. You turn backward. I'm having a rough time, a bad day, and I feel like I'm out of gas? I get out there and I don't need gas no more. I'm hybrid. I got my own little battery pack. I feel like me. I feel free.

* * * * *

What puts gas in your tank, sister? You will need to know.

If we are to get and remain free, Black women and girls must recognize what it looks like when we are moving away from freedom. For me, it looks like disorganization, forgetfulness, avoidance, and a lack of motivation. It looks like overindulging and not treating my body kindly. It looks like isolation from friends and family.

When those things happen, it is time to reclaim myself. Black women and girls must know how to do that. When you have somehow taken the wrong turn on the path to freedom, how do you recalculate and return to the route?

It is important to ask what choices you can make from a place of strength and alrightness to regain your footing. Sometimes it might be as simple as making a decision to reject the strong Black woman caricature by sitting down on a Sunday evening, taking a closer look at your calendar, and identifying things to say no to. It might be booking an appointment with a therapist. What works for you will be personal.

Beatrice

I love being with my family someplace where you don't get a good cell signal. We're not talking about current affairs, family dynamics, anything heavy. It's just blue skies, blue water, and adult beverages all day long. That's freedom. That's when I feel my most free.

I can't live that way all the time, so I prioritize caring for my well-being. I have to take short breaks throughout the day. I meditate in the morning, in the evening, and sometimes after meetings at work, because people get on my last nerves. I started practicing yoga. I curate my media intake like I curate my friends. I go to certain sources, get what I need, and I get out. I don't watch the evening or morning news. And I manage how much TV I watch in general because of all that advertising trying to sell me something by reminding me that my hair doesn't bounce, my skin doesn't glow, and I'm too old to do cartwheels anymore. I don't need that. That's not freedom. That is imprisonment.

I feel more free, more self-possessed, more confident, more self-aware at seventy than I ever did at seventeen or eighteen. The things that I stressed about as a young woman seem unimportant. At seventy, the best thing you can have is your health, your mind, and the ability to go about life as independently as possible. That's freedom.

I started working on me when I was my only vested interest. My family and the people around me became the beneficiaries of that. I didn't want my daughter to be under any of the yokes and shackles of the nonsense I had experienced as a Black woman. I wanted my man to feel free out here in this mess. And I wanted my parents, who were still living at the time, to embrace a new definition of freedom. I found more freedom in being able to help liberate other people. They're better because I'm better and I continue to grow.

The biggest challenge is learning to let go—letting the people around me grow, and grow their way instead of trying to make them grow in my image or in the way I think they should. When you are in the process of moving forward, it's important to recognize who is not ready to come along. I'm not Sisyphus. I'm not going to push your ass. We either move in tandem or you go your way and I hope we meet somewhere, someplace down the line. I mean, that's family. That's friends. That's anybody. We're moving together. We're working together. That's fine. But you need to learn to work through your shit. You need somebody to bounce some ideas off of, I'm your girl. But don't come back to me asking for some help and then we got to talk about it over and over. I'm not that girl. Get a therapist. You've got tools; and if you don't have tools, I can help you find those resources. But work through that shit.

It matters who you let into your life. It matters who you don't. You got to pick who you are around and where they are in their journey and in their season. Some people walk around literally with a cloud burst over their heads all the time. You can feel it. You can sense it. You walk into a room and you just know there's something. You know that they're not connected to source. I can only spend a little bit of time around people like that because they're draining. I protect my energy because you got vampires and vacuums out there, and they'll just try to either tap into it or suck it all up. No, no, no, no, no, I need that. I need my sprinkles, the sunshine, the belief, the fairy dust that I have cultivated over seventy years.

* * * * *

The practice of freedom is not a solitary venture. As an oft-repeated proverb says: if you want to go far, go together. Black women and girls are more likely to commit to a practice of freedom if they are in community with other women and girls similarly dedicated to their own liberation. This is especially true once we recognize that our fates are connected.

Audre Lorde wrote, "I am not free while any woman is unfree, even when her shackles are very different from my own." Our freedom practice can unlock the liberation of our sisters and future generations; our freedom practice feeds on support and sisterhood.

River

My mother is a woman who does not often choose herself. When I was growing up, she would say, "Put your feelings in your back pocket. No one cares about your feelings." I had to evolve out of believing that my needs and wants don't matter—that other folks aren't thinking about me and I shouldn't be, either.

Somebody said that God gives us children to help us finish growing up and healing. Having children helped me begin to question what I was taught about my own worth, because *of course* their feelings matter. My son has a hereditary degenerative condition that caused him to lose his vision at age fourteen. When he was dealing with that, there was no way in hell I was going to stand there and act like his feelings didn't matter.

Around the time my son was diagnosed, I was in the middle of a separation that eventually led to divorce. I was enrolled in a doctoral program. My father was dying. I was trying to navigate a new life working for myself as a consultant. I had a lot of life going on, and a sister friend recommended a fantastic therapist. Entering into that therapeutic relationship was also a game changer. It helped me to pull the curtain back and begin to see that my well-being does matter. It matters a lot.

Liberation is about being able to freely unfold in ways that serve my highest good. Black women are sometimes encouraged to believe that it is selfish to seek our own freedom. But I know that in those moments when I felt myself being liberated, I was serving my son and daughter's highest good, too.

Other women play a role in how we practice freedom or not. I learned from my mother. I learned from my therapist. I learned from the Black women I interviewed as part of my doctoral dissertation. I was studying women who took from five to twenty years to complete a two-year degree program. Those interviews with those women fed me at a time when I was going through it. They told me about making hard choices in life while harder things are happening. I learned about persistence, staying the course, keeping the faith, and staying in flow. These women chose themselves and showed up for themselves under some really difficult circumstances.

A liberation journey takes a village—a community—based on my experience. I've had opportunities to bear witness to women in my circle when they're going through hard times. Navigating successfully takes a level of awareness that is hard to have in isolation. You need a team. I need Team River, whether it's my therapist or my best friend. Those people can see what I can't. Fish don't talk about water. Humans don't talk about air; our bodies are just created to breathe it. I need Team River to make me aware of what I can't see that may be standing in the way of my choosing myself. I need mirror holders to help me see myself.

* * * * *

The first line of Patanjali's *Yoga Sutras* is a reminder of the nature of practice: *Atha Yoganusasanum*, which translates to "Now, the practice of yoga." The "now" keeps us forever in the present moment. We practice yoga now and now and now. In the same way, Black women and girls must make a decision to recommit to freedom and choose ourselves in each moment.

The pressure on Black women to conform to societal pressures is relentless. We must spot broken narratives, unearth and celebrate our true selves, and weigh the costs of our liberation, again and again.

Now, freedom.

Now, freedom.

Now, freedom.

HOW TO SPOT
The Path Away from Freedom

Ask yourself these questions to determine if you are no longer practicing freedom:

- How do I feel? Do I feel centered, inspired, and motivated, or overwhelmed and trapped?

- Am I intentional about treating myself well? Am I eating, exercising, and taking my medicine?

- Am I rooted in my alrightness?

- Are my expectations of myself realistic or based on a belief that Black women are unbreakable martyrs?

- If someone I love—a friend or family member—were moving like I am, would I be concerned about her?

DO THIS
Planning for Hard Times

In your journal, write about how you will recognize when you have fallen off the path to freedom and how you will recalculate your route back.

READ THIS
Freedom Literature

Lisa, a woman you will meet in the next chapter, says that she stays on the path to liberation by reading "freedom literature," books that remind her of her alrightness and humanity. Here are her selections:

- *Sisters of the Yam: Black Women and Self-Discovery* by bell hooks

- *The Temple of My Familiar* by Alice Walker

- Anything by Toni Morrison (the GOAT of Black women's literature—*all* literature)

- *We Speak Your Names: A Celebration* by Pearl Cleage

And here is one from me:

- "The Bridge Poem" by Donna Kate Rushin

CHAPTER 9

See Free Black Women Everywhere

I think that Black sisterhood could very well be the key to Black unity. African-American women, we've been the rocks of the race. Having nothing but love between us is like the key to the whole community really coming together in love.

—VIVIAN GREEN

Like a lot of Black women, I wear a silk or satin bonnet at night to maintain moisture in my highly textured hair and to preserve my hairstyle. I don't wear my bonnet or any other sleepwear outside of my house, so I don't run the risk of a tap on the shoulder from "Auntie" Mo'Nique.

Back in 2021, the comedian sparked a weeks-long public debate about young Black women's comportment, after she spotted young Black women in the airport wearing pajama pants, flip flops, and bonnets. She was so aghast that she took to Instagram to deliver a PSA:

> I've been seeing it not just at the airport. I've been seeing it at the store, at the mall. . . . When did we lose our pride in representing ourselves? When did we slip away from "let me make sure I'm presentable when I leave my home"? I'm not saying you don't have pride but the representation that you're showing, someone will have to ask you to know if you have it.

Mo'Nique warned that she would step to any Black woman she encountered "in the streets, in the airports, in the Walmart and you got a bonnet on and you got slippers on and you looking like what the fuck." And she urged other "wise" Black women of a certain age to do the same.

> That may be a part of us helping our community, because if you look like you don't give a damn, how you gonna be treated? When I say "Hey, Queen," I can only say it to the sistas that it belongs to. Because a lot of us are still in queen training. So if you're in queen training stop being fearful of taking your position. Queens don't walk around in bonnets, and head scarves and slippers and pajamas. That's for the house. When you go outside, represent you, baby . . . like you are worthy and you deserve the title of "Hey, Queen."

Look, I think wearing bonnets and sleep clothes outside of the house is tacky. Perhaps I am simply a product of my generation (X). But I won't be tapping any young Black women on the shoulder at the airport or anywhere else.

The bonnet debate is an example of how Black women are judged harshly and given little grace. At my Big 12 college (Go, Cyclones!), it was not uncommon to see my mostly White fellow women students around campus with wet hair and men's boxer shorts over leggings. Fashionable? No. Tacky? Maybe. Lazy? Probably. But who cares? Those women were on campus to get an education. No one doubted their personal pride. No one suggested that other people would be justified in treating these women poorly. No one suggested that other people would be justified in treating all White women poorly just because of a few young women's sartorial choices. No one suggested that the long work of women's suffragists like Elizabeth Cady Stanton and Susan B. Anthony was for naught because young White women in the late eighties/early nineties were wearing boxers instead of bustles. The idea is absurd. And in a society with increasingly expansive and relaxed ideas about dress, it is worth asking why the choices of Black women are uniquely concerning.

Again, Black women and girls are alright. We have human value and agency. We do not need to *earn* value by wearing the right things in public. It is racist and sexist to demand that Black women alone conform to arbitrary standards of comportment not just to receive respect or avoid public lashings on the internet, but to access healthcare and education for our children.

In 2023, James Madison High School in Houston issued a dress code for parents in which it banned, among other things, satin caps or bonnets.[1] In the same year, an Ohio dentist issued a similar dress code for patients.[2] It is interesting to note that both James Madison High School's principal and the Ohio dentist are Black women.

Too often we are at the vanguard of policing our sisters. And even our rules for each other can be arbitrary. It was not lost on some folks that Mo'Nique recorded the video scolding young Black women for improper public dress while wearing what appeared to be a bathrobe, which leaves me to wonder if the comedian's rant was less about teaching proper bearing and more about remaking other women in her image.

Dawnie

I come from North Florida and two very different Black families. My father's side was highly educated. My paternal grandparents went to college in the 1930s and had pretty much the best jobs you could hope to get at that time as Black folks in the South. My grandmother was a maternity nurse and my grandfather was a football coach and teacher. My mother's side sort of lived as the money came; it often did not.

As different as those two sides of my family were, there was one thing that they had in common: they were both hyperaware of presentation. On my father's side of the family, it was very much like you speak properly when you spend time with them. They would correct your language—that kind of thing. My maternal grandmother was very much about what she saw as appropriate female comportment. Proper foundation garments—nothing jiggling or hanging out. Not being loud. No rollers in your hair outside of the house. Behaving as a lady should. I learned from her and other Black women that being demure as a Black woman is how you earn respect from the community and from men. It is how Black women get ahead. I remember well how older Black women would talk badly about the women they felt didn't carry themselves right.

I adore and respect my family very much, but a lot of their beliefs about how Black people should show up in public were rooted in respectability politics. I haven't been able to turn that off. I'm a pearl clutcher. There's a feeling that I've learned to recognize when I am triggered by a Black woman showing up in a way I've been trained to view as "wrong." Black women can be extra hard on each other, even when other groups of people display the same damn behavior as we do. I learned in therapy to be mindful. The important thing is for me not to immediately jump to conclusions about who a woman is and what her life is like because I really don't know. I don't know that I've been able to completely change my programming, but I recognize it.

Watching the way younger Black women move is inspiring. They seem to be claiming the freedom to embrace multiple facets of themselves, whether it is their intellectualism or their sexuality. They have confidence and a lack of concern over what other people are saying or thinking, especially over what White people might be saying or thinking.

Sometimes I look at old pictures of myself in my twenties and I feel a little sadness. I was wearing all these big, boxy, baggy things. I mean, that was the style in the nineties. But I am not sure if my choices were about the style of the time or conditioning that told me I shouldn't be too "loud" in my appearance or too "out there." I'm not sure whether my choices as a young woman were driven by what I preferred or what my family taught me society preferred of women like me. Now I'm in my forties and, you know, your body starts to change and things don't bounce back. . . . Maybe I could have enjoyed my young body more. Maybe I could have been a little freer.

I was promoting my novel *The Final Revival of Opal and Nev*, which is about a Black woman navigating the music industry in the 1970s. This interviewer asked me to talk about women in today's industry. She wanted me to talk about how today's Black women artists have to "basically hit the [stripper] pole" to have an impact. I had to stop and think about my response to that interviewer's very loaded questions. Those are not the kind of artists that I really like or relate to. Their choices are not mine. But not everything is meant for me or for kids. And I know that being in the prime of your life and feeling sexually free can be empowering for some women. That's okay. You know what I mean? And the music industry *is* very sexualized, but not just for Black women.

* * * * *

We fret over what our sisters do because we believe it will influence how society sees us. We are not wrong. People who harbor racist values see us as interchangeable; they place the imagined sins of one of us on all of us. And patriarchy encourages women to see each other as enemies and competitors. So we watch our sisters to make sure they don't do anything we wouldn't do. Black women are connected, but not like that. Sister, we must know better. There are better ways to teach younger generations about how to show up than denigrating public discourse and arbitrary rules that target them.

Nikki Myers, the internationally recognized yoga therapist, Somatic Experiencing practitioner, and certified Addictions Recovery Specialist who you met in chapter 6, said to me, "One of the things that I've come to learn about liberation is that it really is about interdependence rather than independence. My liberation is very much intertwined with yours and with nature and with all of those things. We're all made of the same stuff, right? We may look like individual things, but really we are not. In order for me to have freedom, you have to have it, too."

We are tethered. And our role is not to be hammers that bludgeon our sisters into submission to society's mercurial rules. Our role is to walk with fellow Black women and girls to freedom. Our personal liberation work sets the stage for that.

Lisa

To support Black women's liberation, I had to first cultivate my own freedom. Invest in it. I had to challenge and heal the things in my life that made me not free. I had to be honest with myself about where my hurts were.

From four to eighteen, I was involved in a Pentecostal cult with my mom. She liked to call it a church; it was a cult to me. It was anti-woman, anti-Black, anti-anything but religion. It took the Bible and weaponized it against us—against women. When I got pregnant at sixteen, my mother's pastor threatened to kick her out of the church if I got an abortion. I had my child and gave the baby up for adoption.

Experiencing the horrible and sexist way women and girls were treated in that church led by Black men prompted me to move, for a time, like a living "fuck you" to the church, to Black men, to patriarchy, to religion. I thought that was freedom, but it wasn't. I got free when I came to understand that I didn't have to live in active opposition to all those things. I could just be a fully functioning, liberated Black woman. I could live abundantly on my own terms and let go of that garbage. And, through my work as a therapist, I could help other Black women do the same.

I also had to face my fears about the cost of free Black womanhood. Fear is the main driver of remaining in darkness and remaining aligned with people and things that are antithetical to what you want. We are afraid of what happens when our closest friends start being like, "Who the fuck are you?" It doesn't feel good when your mama is still dedicated and intentional about *not* being free. You can find yourself alone. I once had a client quit therapy. She said, "The things that are happening inside of me because of our work together are creating chaos for me at home." She could not financially afford to leave a husband who was abusive and neglectful, but her growing mental freedom made it hard to stay. In our freedom, we can make different, healthy relationships, but I've made peace with the fact that most women aren't going to do this work. It's too hard. It's scary. It ain't for the weak.

I know that Black women cannot live based on the [biased] things people have said about us. Freedom, for me, means that

I get to show up in my fullest humanity, no matter how that looks, without undue judgment. It means I get to be intentional about my life and make choices based on what I want and need. It means I get to live out my soul's work here.

I want Black women to start being like, "Listen, this is how I want to live, and this is how I'm going to live." I want us to be free to say, "No. I can't. I won't." When I accept that I can do the things that feel good and natural to me, then I love it when other Black women do the things that feel good and natural to them.

* * * * *

We are examples for our sisters not based on whether we show up at the airport in a bonnet or fresh blowout, but based on how we honor and nurture our collective freedom. The work of seeing our sisters as alright and helping them to see themselves as alright is vital. And this is how we ensure that Black women and girls stay free over generations.

Young Black women and girls don't need us to tap them on the shoulder. They see us. They see what we do. They see what we say about each other. They see how free we live and how free we are willing to give other women permission to live.

Peyton

Freedom is the opportunity to be fully me—my whole Black woman self. It is walking into a room without first thinking about what the room is going to think of me, just like a cisgender straight White man would. I feel that kind of freedom when I'm in my community. Like, I went to a poetry slam last week and it was amazing! There were a lot of Black folks there—just unapologetic Black excellence. Black girls in waist beads and head wraps. Amazing poets just speaking their truth, speaking their magic. And I was like, *This is liberation! This is what being free is.*

I graduated a year ago from a very White private school. It was hard to find community there. It was hard to find liberation. It's hard to be free when you're the only Black girl in your class. When you're navigating racist stuff over and over again at a place that can't or won't handle it. When you're in a competitive and cliquey environment. When you're in a White space and there is extra pressure to conform to the majority. When a lot of Black students are on scholarship and you are not. I tried really hard not to be the loud Black girl in class. I was still known as the loud Black girl because I couldn't help calling out racist stuff. That's just who I am. They thought I was loud, but I could have been much louder; I could have been calling them out on more bull crap, for sure. I felt like I had to hide myself when I was there. I felt stifled. I didn't feel free. And maybe that's part of why I haven't found my "tribe" among Black women my age yet.

I do know what supportive relations between Black women look like. I learned that watching older women: my mother and her friends. A lot of them are Black woman creators—writers and artists. I see how they interact with each other and I can get their advice. I see how they do what they want. Right now, every time I call my mom, she's in a different country. She is living her best life and I truly and deeply love that for her. That is where I have found community and, like, a blueprint for relating to other Black women. Support for other Black women's freedom looks like empathy and kindness, understanding and trust. It's knowing that every woman is going through her own ... whatever ... and being able to approach other women with kindness no matter what. I'm working to be that kind of support to other Black women my age. As cliche as it sounds, I believe I can do anything I want because I've seen other Black women do that. They face backlash and repercussions, but they still proceed. They still push through.

Right now, I'm working on myself, figuring out what is necessary for me and what I need in my life. I've been hurt by many people, but I realize that I have relied too much on other people to get my own happiness, and that's chaining me to other people. So let me stop doing that. I found an amazing therapist, a Black woman. And I'm working on self-love.

✳ ✳ ✳ ✳ ✳

We are too often complicit in the bondage of our sisters. This is our dirty secret. It is often mothers who first caution daughters against being "fast," grandmamas who warn girls in from the sun lest they become too dark, Black women who pick at and bully other Black women online. A dear friend once told me, "We cannot see our sisters in any greater light than we can see ourselves." Sister, the individual liberation of Black women is the gateway to collective freedom. The steps I offer in this book are designed to bring us to a space where we can love each other more fully by loving ourselves first.

But, in loving our sisters, we must be able to appraise them without attachment—that is, we must see other Black women as interconnected but autonomous even from ourselves. Another principle I discovered through yoga practice is that of *aparigraha*, one of the moral observances often defined as non-attachment or non-possessiveness. In the *Bhagavad Gita*, Krishna counsels, "Let your concern be with the action alone, and never with the fruits of action. Do not let the results of your action be your motive, and do not be attached to inaction."

We cannot be attached to how other Black women and girls live their lives. We cannot hope that our sisters will remake themselves in society's image or *our* image. We are not, I think, our sisters' keepers, we are our sisters' companions and co-conspirators. We love. We nurture. We support. We help our sisters excavate their authentic selves. And we let our sisters be free.

DO THIS
Explore Your Own Bias

In your journal, write about your feelings for the high-profile Black women below. (Feel free to add your own.) How might your negative and positive feelings be colored by bias?

- Meghan Thee Stallion, rapper

- Michelle Obama, former United States First Lady

- Laverne Cox, actress and LGBTQ activist

- Nene Leakes, reality TV star

- Kamala Harris, United States vice president

- Ciara, singer

Also, write about how it feels to be supported in your alrightness by other women. How might you do a better job of seeing free Black women everywhere?

DO THIS
Be a Better Sister

Are you judging your sisters fairly? Some questions to ask:

- Do I expect my sister to make the same choices as I would?

- Is my assessment of my sister rooted in foundational stereotypes of Black women?

- Am I centering my sister's alrightness or approaching her as someone in need of fixing?

- Am I concerned about how my sister's actions will look to White people or others outside our community?

- Have I listened to my sister to understand her experience and her needs?

- Am I am making assumptions about my sister based on incomplete information?

EPILOGUE

Free your mind and
the rest will follow.
—EN VOGUE

S ister:

Your freedom can begin in no other place than inside you.

Feminist scholar bell hooks wrote, "If any [woman] feels she needs anything beyond herself to legitimate and validate her existence, she is already giving away her power to be self-defining, her agency." bell is right, as she was on so many things.

No one has more capacity to truly see you than YOU.

Other people may render you a caricature. You must always know the fully drawn real woman behind the distortion.

"[You] wear the mask that grins and lies" to protect your identity. You must always know the real face underneath the disguise.

When you can recognize the conqueror's poison
before you sip it;

when you know who you are, absent the hum of
misogynoir;

127

when you love who you are—even the hard parts;

when you are clear about what parts of yourself you can afford to gamble with and which you cannot;

when you have made a commitment to choose yourself and your well-being again and again;

then you will be free.

And when you can see me, sister, in all my alrightness,

then we will be free together.

GLOSSARY

The language in this book reflects what I think it must be like having a conversation with authentic me—a little yogi; a lot of feminist; a dash of woo-woo; some Black girl speak and up-South vernacular; a midwesternism or two; a soupçon of smarty-pants and "if you know you know"; and humor. If, while reading this book, you wondered, *What the hell is Tamara talking about?* or, better, *I want to further explore what the hell Tamara is talking about*, this glossary will help you.

Act Like a Lady, Think Like a Man A 2014 book that turned thrice-married comedian Steve Harvey into an improbable relationship guru. The book warns women away from "too much" independence and achievement, asserting that modern women must learn to be more submissive and "ladylike" to attract men who must play traditional dominant roles. One of only two books I have ever thrown across a room.

Ayurveda Alternative health system with roots in the Indian subcontinent. Includes practices such as yoga, meditation, medicinal herbs, and oils.

Bhagavad Gita A seven-hundred-verse Hindi scripture that is part of the epic tale Mahabharata. Spiritual guidance on duty and purpose is delivered on a bloody battlefield by Krishna, an avatar of the god Vishnu, to warrior Prince Arjuna.

Big Momma, Madea, Rasputia et al. Caricatures of Black women made famous by Black male comedians in drag. Martin Lawrence introduced Big Momma in his 2000 movie *Big Momma's House*. Tyler Perry has portrayed Madea on stage and the big screen since the 1990s. Rasputia terrorized the main character in Eddie Murphy's 2007 *Norbit*. The characters are three of many portrayals of Black womanhood, presented as Black entertainment, which reinforce stereotypes of Black women as unattractive, large, loud, aggressive, and sexually promiscuous.

Colorism Prejudice against people with dark skin— typically among people of the same ethnic or racial group. Based on the idea that skin color and features most proximate to Whiteness are most desirable and marks of superior intelligence, beauty, and value. There is no such thing as "reverse colorism."

Eight Limbs of Yoga Yoga is much more than physical postures. In the Yoga Sutras of Patanjali (see below), Patanjali explains the eight "limbs" of classical yoga, including yama (restraints), niyama (observances), asana (posture), pranayama (breath control), pratyahara (withdrawal of the senses), dharana (concentration), dhyana (meditation), and samadhi (pure contemplation). Practicing yoga is to incorporate all eight limbs.

FUPA Fat upper-pussy area—popular slang referring to a woman's often rounded lower abdomen.

Zora Neale Hurston American author and anthropologist. Her works include the foundational *Their Eyes Were Watching God*. Hurston also traveled the South and Caribbean, recording local cultural practices and folklore.

Jezebel One of the four core stereotypes about Black women. The Jezebel stereotype suggests that Black women are sexually immoral and promiscuous.

Laid edges A smooth hairline, free of fuzzies, frizzies, kinks, and curls.

Mahabharata A major Hindu epic that tells the story of the Kurukshetra War between the Kauravas and Pandavas, two branches of the same family. The Mahabharata contains the Bhagavad Gita, as well as other spiritual and philosophical material.

Mammy One of the four core stereotypes about Black women. The Mammy stereotype suggests that Black women are meant to happily serve others without regard for their own needs or desires.

Matriarch One of the four core stereotypes about Black women. The Matriarch stereotype suggests that single Black mothers have ruined their communities through their promiscuity, aggression, and independence and by refusing to be chaste and submissive to male leadership.

Maybelle's Cabin My favorite cozy cabin getaway spot in Brown County, Indiana. (They got tiny horses, y'all!)

Middle Passage The forced voyage of enslaved men and women across the Atlantic Ocean to the West Indies and Americas.

Misogynoir A term coined by Black feminist scholar Moya Bailey to describe the particular misogyny, coupled with racism, endured by Black women.

"De mules of de world" The iconic line from Zora Neale Hurston's book *Their Eyes Were Watching God,* describing the mythology around strength that positions Black women as burden bearers.

Patanjali Mystic and philosopher believed to have written the Yoga Sutras, a collection of truths about the theory and practice of yoga.

Phat ass v. Fat ass Modern society loves a "phat" ass—1990s slang for highly attractive or "pretty, hot, and tempting"—but abhors a fat ass, unless it is fat in the right way, which is not fat at all but generous and round. Just know that Black women's asses get a lot of undue scrutiny.

Reiki A healing technique using light touch to promote relaxation and well-being.

Respectability politics A political strategy where marginalized groups consciously mimic the values, beliefs, and customs of the majority to better assimilate and gain social mobility.

Kevin Samuels The late self-styled "image consultant" who rose to popularity by dispensing misogynistic dating advice on the internet.

Sapphire One of the four core stereotypes about Black women. The Sapphire stereotype suggests that Black women are unnaturally strong, hearty and aggressive. While the stereotype is rooted in antebellum America, the name "Sapphire" comes from the nagging wife in the mid-twentieth-century radio and TV program *Amos and Andy*.

Big Mama Thornton Six-foot, queer, Black, blues badass who sang the song "Hound Dog" three years before Elvis Presley.

Upanishads Hindu text detailing rites, incantations, esoteric knowledge, and a vision of an interconnected universe.

"We Wear the Mask" A 1895 poem written by Paul Lawrence Dunbar, describing how Black Americans often must hide their true selves and feelings from the wider world. The poem begins, "We wear the mask that grins and lies. It hides our cheeks and shades our eyes. This debt we pay to human guile. With torn and bleeding hearts we smile. And mouth with myriad subtleties."

Yoga Sutras of Patanjali The foundational text
of yogic philosophy, which includes 195 statements on the
theory and practice of yoga.

NOTES

PREFACE

1 Josh Levin, "The Real Story of Linda Taylor, America's Original Welfare Queen," *Slate*, December 19, 2013, https://www.slate.com/articles/news _and_politics/history/2013/12/linda_taylor_welfare_queen_ronald _reagan_made_her_a_notorious_american_villain.html.

2 Tamara Winfrey Harris, *The Sisters Are Alright: Changing the Broken Narrative of Black Women in America*, 2nd ed. (Oakland, CA: Berrett-Koehler, 2021), 9–10.

3 Juliet Macur, "Simone Biles Is Withdrawing from the Olympic All-Around Gymnastics Competition," *New York Times*, July 28, 2021, https://www.nytimes.com/2021/07/28/sports/olympics/simone-biles -out.html#:~:text=Simone%20Biles%20is%20withdrawing%20from, continue%20without%20risking%20severe%20injury.

4 Brenley Goertzen, "Charlie Kirk, Piers Morgan Slam Simone Biles as a 'Selfish Sociopath' and 'Shame to the Country,'" *Salon*, July 28, 2021, https://www.salon.com/2021/07/charlie-kirk-piers-morgan-slam -simone-biles-shes-a-selfish-sociopath-shame-to-the-country/.

5 Matthew Futterman, "Naomi Osaka Quits the French Open after News Conference Dispute," *New York Times*, May 31, 2021, https://www .nytimes.com/2021/05/31/sports/tennis/naomi-osaka-quits-french-open -depression.html.

6 Lateshia Beachum, "Black Female Athletes Are Setting Records—and Now Leading Conversations about Mental Health," *Washington Post*, August 2, 2021, https://www.washingtonpost.com/sports/2021/07/30 /biles-osaka-mental-black-women/.

NOTES

CHAPTER 1

1 Jazmin Brooks, "This African Braiding Technique Was Created by Our Ancestors to Help Prevent Hunger during Slavery," *Essence*, October 23, 2020, https://www.essence.com/hair/african-braiding-technique-rice -hunger-slavery/.

2 Haben Kelati, "Blues Singer 'Big Mama' Thornton Had a Hit with 'Hound Dog.' Then Elvis Came Along.," *Washington Post*, March 1, 2021, https://www.washingtonpost.com/lifestyle/kidspost/blues-singer -big-mama-thornton-had-a-hit-with-hound-dog-then-elvis-came-along /2021/02/23/60c36a04-6764-11eb-8468-21bc48f07fe5_story.html.

3 Kat Stoeffel, "There's a Change.org Petition about Blue Ivy's Hair," *The Cut*, June 10, 2014, https://www.thecut.com/2014/06/changeorg -petition-about-blue-ivys-hair.html.

4 Edward W. Morris, "'Ladies' or 'Loudies'?: Perceptions and Experiences of Black Girls in Classrooms," *Youth & Society* 38, no. 4 (2007): 490–515, https://doi.org/10.1177/0044118X06296778.

5 Clemence Michallon, "Dress Code Discrimination: Black Girls Are More Likely to Be Disciplined for Clothing at School than Their Peers— Because 'Adults See Them as Older and More Sexual,'" *Daily Mail*, May 1, 2018, https://www.dailymail.co.uk/femail/article-5679159 /Black-girls-likely-peers-dress-coded-school.html.

CHAPTER 2

1 Jocelyn Frye, "Rejecting Business as Usual: Improving Employment Outcomes and Economic Security for Black Women," issue brief, National Partnership for Women & Families, September 25, 2023, https://nationalpartnership.org/report/improving-employment -outcomes-economic-security-for-black-women/.

2 National Women's Law Center, "In 2021, More than 12 Million Women and Girls Lacked Health Insurance; Poverty Rates Still Adversely Affected Women of Color at Higher Rates than Their White Counterparts; and the Wage Gap Has for Women Overall Widened to 84 Cents," press release, September 14, 2022, https://nwlc.org/press-release/in -2021-more-than-12-million-women-and-girls-lacked-health-insurance -poverty-rates-still-adversely-affected-women-of-color-at-higher-rates -than-their-white-counterparts-and-the-wage-gap-has-for-wom/#:~ :text=Poverty%20rates%20were%20worse%20for,lived%20in %20poverty%20in%202021.

3 Chris Martinez et al., "Release: Nearly Two-Thirds of Mothers Continue to Be Family Breadwinners, Black Mothers Are Far More Likely to Be Breadwinners," Center for American Progress, November 6, 2023, https://www.americanprogress.org/press/release-nearly-two-thirds -mothers-continue-family-breadwinners-black-mothers-far-likely -breadwinners/.

4 Associated Press and Kat Stafford, "Why Do So Many Black Women Die in Pregnancy? One Reason: Doctors Don't Take Them Seriously," AP News, July 14, 2021, https://projects.apnews.com/features/2023 /from-birth-to-death/black-women-maternal-mortality-rate.html#:~ :text=Black%20women%20have%20the%20highest,for%20Disease %20Control%20and%20Prevention.

5 W. McNabb, M. Quinn, and J. Tobian, "Diabetes in African American Women: The Silent Epidemic," NIH National Library of Medicine 3, no. 3–4 (1997): 275–300, https://pubmed.ncbi.nlm.nih.gov/9426497/.

6 Alexa Spencer, "Here's Why Depression in Black Women Might Be Overlooked by Doctors," Word In Black, January 17, 2023, https:/ /wordinblack.com/2023/01/heres-why-depression-in-black-women -might-be-overlooked-by-doctors/#:~:text=Exposure%20to%20racism %20and%20other,may%20go%20overlooked%20by%20doctors.

CHAPTER 3

1 "The Women & Girls Index," Lilly Family School of Philanthropy, accessed November 7, 2023, https://philanthropy.iupui.edu/institutes /womens-philanthropy-institute/research/wgi.html.

2 Indiana State Data," Status of Women in the States, October 26, 2015, https://statusofwomendata.org/explore-the-data/state-data/indiana/.

3 Publication, *Landscape Study of Women's Funds and Foundations Part I*, 2022.

4 Mirae Kim and Bo Li, "Nonprofits Led by People of Color Get Less Funding than Others," The Chronicle of Philanthropy, March 10, 2023, https://www.philanthropy.com/article/nonprofits-led-by-people-of -color-get-less-funding-than-others.

CHAPTER 7

1 Jocelyn Frye, "Rejecting Business as Usual: Improving Employment Outcomes and Economic Security for Black Women," National

Partnership for Women & Families, September 25, 2023, https:/
/nationalpartnership.org/report/improving-employment-outcomes
-economic-security-for-black-women/#:~:text=In%20June%202023
%2C%20Black%20women's,Population%20Survey%20Table%20A
%2D2.

2   Institute for Women's Policy Research, "Women of Color," Status of
Women in the States report, June 1, 2015, https://statusofwomendata
.org/women-of-color/.

3   William Lutz, "Black Women Earn Less than White Men in Every
State, Will Not Reach Pay Equity with White Men until 2144, According
to a New IWPR Fact Sheet," Institute for Women's Policy Research,
August 3, 2023, https://iwpr.org/black-women-earn-less-than-white
-men-in-every-state-will-not-reach-pay-equity-with-white-men-until
-2144-according-to-a-new-iwpr-fact-sheet/#:~:text=IWPR%20Fact
%20Sheet-,Black%20Women%20Earn%20Less%20than%20
White%20Men%20in%20Every%20State,a%20New%20IWPR
%20Fact%20Sheet&text=Washington%2C%20D.C.%20%E2%80
%94%20Black%20women%20earned,Pay%20Day%20July%20
27%2C%202023.

4   Nina Banks, "Black Women's Labor Market History Reveals Deep-
Seated Race and Gender Discrimination," Economic Policy Institute,
February 19, 2019, https://www.epi.org/blog/black-womens-labor
-market-history-reveals-deep-seated-race-and-gender-discrimination/.

5   Tamara E. Holmes, "How to Get around 'Black Tax' and Protect Your
Emotional Health at Work," *Essence*, October 27, 2020, https://www
.essence.com/news/money-career/black-women-burden-success-black
-tax-emotional-health/.

CHAPTER 9

1   Nadra Nittle, "A High School's Dress Code for Parents Sparked Backlash.
The Principal Is Standing by It.," Vox, May 7, 2019, https://www.vox.com
/the-goods/2019/5/7/18532416/james-madison-high-school-dress-code.

2   Nicole Duncan-Smith, "'No Bonnets, No House Shoes, No Pajama Bot-
toms': Dress Code at Dentist's Office Causes a Stir on Twitter. Some Say
It's Anti-Black and 'Prejudice against Poor People,'" *Atlanta Black Star*,
May 21, 2023, https://atlantablackstar.com/2023/05/21/dress-codes-are
-historically-racist-sign-banning-hair-bonnets-shoes-pajamas-at-ohio
-dentists-office-sparks-debate-outrage-on-twitter-some-say-its-anti-black/.

ACKNOWLEDGMENTS

To Mommy and Daddy for their love and support and for nurturing my love of words, writing, and stories.

To my husband, LaMarl, for our lovely journey together. I will remember it for both of us.

To the women who trusted me enough to share their stories here with honesty and vulnerability.

To the sisters who, in this hardest moment of life, have held me down, lifted me up, and often made me laugh until it hurt: River, Deesha, Patrice, Carolyn, Tyffani, Tiffany, Audrey, Carol, Delisa, Donisha, Lacy, and so many others.

To Deesha, again, for pushing me toward radical honesty in my writing and for modeling a joyous creative life.

To bell, Audre, Zora, Alice, Toni, Kate, and all the other writers of the Black femme sacred texts.

To the sister yogi, whose name I do not remember, who taught class on Saturday mornings at the little studio that is probably no longer above the Mellow Yellow on 53rd Street in Hyde Park (Chicago) for introducing me to the expansiveness of yoga practice.

ACKNOWLEDGMENTS

To Neal, Jeevan, and the team at Berrett-Koehler Publishers for caring about these Black women's stories as much as I do and treating them and me with celebration and respect.

Thank you.

I love you.

You help me be free.

May you be free, too.

INDEX

A

"acceptable"
  attempts to meet definition of, xiv, xi, 7–8, 52
  for Black hair, 69
  quietness as, 5–6
  romantic partnership as, 92
  as taught by elders, 47, 67
acquiescence, xv
Act Like a Lady, Think Like a Man (Harvey), 129
activism, 67, 103
African ancestry, 79
aggressiveness, 76
aging, 105
ahimsa, 93–94
allies, 44, 49, 67
alrightness
  vs. broken narratives, 9
  decolonization via, 11
  as flawed and divine, 3–4
  as inherent, 115
  policing vs., 47
  practicing, 12
  self-love for, 73–74
  sisterhood of, 121
  truly believing, 24
  uncovering your, 61
Amara La Negra, 69
American Methodist Church, 62–64

anger, 66, 76
anxiety, 33, 34, 37, 77, 87, 99
asses, 132
authentic self
  as alright and divine, 4
  being your, xv–xvi, 12, 102
  and boundaries, 67
  celebrating, 11
  centering, 103, 109
  cost of being, 84, 90, 94
  describing the life of, 71
  freedom for/as, 11, 14–18, 54, 127–128
  hiding your, xiii, xiv–xv
  intentional compromise of, 86–87
  love of, 73–74, 96
  in the Methodist church, 62–64
  rituals of loving, 25–26
  in romantic relationships, 91–93
  vs. small self, 64
  uncovering your, 61, 64
  wholeness of, 74–75, 80
avatars, 81
Ayurveda, 129

B

Bambara, Toni Cade, 83
barriers, structural, 18, 84
beauty standards, xii, 48–49
beliefs, 24

INDEX

health
    breath for, 32
    and expressing anger, 66
    and hierarchy of needs, 89
    via honoring entire self, 74
    meditation and, 33
    mental, 50–51, 87, 89, 99
    physical, 29, 90
    sacrifice of, 90
    and self-suppression, 87
    workplace costs to, 99
healthcare, 16–17
heartbreak, 22
heteronormativity, 46–47
hierarchy of needs, 89
history
    of chattel slavery, 41–43
    European colonial, xii
    power of surviving, 4
homosexuality, 46–47
hooks, bell, 19, 111, 127
humanity, 88, 89, 96, 121
Hurston, Zora Neale, 43, 70, 131, 132
hypervigilance, 99

I

identity
    affirming personal, 15
    cultural, 79
    freedom of, 17–18
    and internalized shame, 52
    sacrificing parts of, 85–87
    uncovering your true, 57, 64–65
    wholeness of, 74–75
Inner Engineering: A Yogi's Guide to Joy (Vasadev), 97
inner work, 103, 120
intentionality, 26
interdependence, 78, 79, 119
internalized bias, ix, 44
isolation, 98

J

James Madison High School, 115
Jezebel stereotype, xii, 42, 54, 58, 131
journaling, 34, 55–56, 71, 81, 98, 103, 110
joy, 28–29, 78, 103, 104
judgment, 125
Just Mercy (Stevenson), 74

K

Kwanzaa, 78–79

L

"Ladies or Loudies?" (Morris), 5
leadership
    male, in the church, 45–46
    and self-love, 102–103
    by women of color, 22–23
letting go, 106
liberation, Black women's
    in community, ix–x, 105–109, 123–124
    cost of, 11, 67, 83–84
    defined, 14–18
    embracing, xv–xvi
    and expressing anger, 66
    modeling, 67
    mutuality in, 119
    poll on, 7
    practicing, 34, 102
    public examples of, xv
    via self-love, 24–25
    six pillars of, 11–12
    stories of, 70–71
    universal nurturing of, 12
    from White sexist society, 9
Liberation Walk, ix
life
    breath as, 30
    of choice, 121

ABOUT THE AUTHOR

 **Tamara Winfrey Harris** is a writer who specializes in the ever-evolving space where current events, politics, and pop culture intersect with race and gender. She says, "I want to tell the stories of Black women and girls, and deliver the truth to all those folks who got us twisted—tangled up in racist and sexist lies. I want my writing to advocate for my sisters. We are better than alright. We are amazing."

Tamara has been published in media outlets, including the *New York Times*, the *Atlantic, Cosmopolitan, New York Magazine, Ms. Magazine*, and the *Los Angeles Times*. Her award-winning first book, *The Sisters Are Alright: Changing the Broken Narrative of Black Women in America*, was published by Berrett-Koehler in 2015 and called "a myth-busting portrait of Black women in America" by the *Washington Post*. Her sophomore effort, *Dear Black Girl: Letters from Your Sisters on Stepping into Your Power*, also from Berrett-Koehler, debuted in March 2021.

Tamara's work also appears in *The Lemonade Reader: Beyoncé, Black Feminism, and Spirituality* (Routledge,

2019); *The Burden: African Americans and the Enduring Impact of Slavery* (Wayne State University Press, 2018); *Black in the Middle: An Anthology of the Black Midwest* (Black Belt Publishing, 2020); and other books.

Tamara serves as president of Women's Fund of Central Indiana, which convenes, invests, and advocates so all who identify as women and girls living in Central Indiana have an equitable opportunity to reach their full potential, no matter their race, place, or identity.

Tamara is a Reiki Master and registered yoga instructor. She says, "I want to share the healing practices that I have learned with people who are chronically disregarded and oppressed in spaces that are safe for them—especially my sisters because they deserve peace." To fulfill this goal, Tamara co-founded River & Tamara, an initiative that provides space for Black women to focus on their well-being and immerse themselves in healing practices. She is also co-founder of the Black Women's Writing Society, which makes space for Black women of all ages to practice their craft and learn from established, poets, journalists, playwrights, and authors.

Tamara is a native of Gary, Indiana, and a proud member of Alpha Kappa Alpha, Sorority, Inc., and The Links Incorporated. She lives outside of Indianapolis with her husband, LaMarl, and two fractious kitties, Jinx and Magick.

ABOUT THE COVER

It is important to Tamara that her books reflect not just her own creativity, but the artistry of other Black women. The covers of *The Sisters Are Alright* and *Dear Black Girl* were designed by Black women artists. The cover of this book was designed by Naomi Silverio.

Naomi is a Dominican illustrator and designer passionate about portraiture and hand lettering. She loves bright colors and pulls inspiration from the things that make her laugh. She currently designs books at Macmillan Children's Publishing Group.

Naomi writes:

There was one thing I felt was the most important while working on this cover, aside from making sure that it properly portrays the kind of book this is: it was making sure our character looked like someone who truly had the Black woman's guide to getting free and could pass it along to someone else. Growing up in a city like NYC means meeting all kinds of people from all different walks of life, but not all advice or words of encouragement can apply to all situations. And that's OK! Sometimes you need to hear different things at different moments and even if the support isn't perfect, the sentiment counts.

ABOUT THE COVER

While I worked on the cover, I kept thinking, *Who is someone I'd go to for advice and what does that person look like?* Surprisingly, the answer felt easier to find than I thought. As a Black woman myself, it was other women who looked just like me—women like my mom, my friends, and even their moms. People who are having or have had similar experiences to mine yet would still know how to share a lesson that anyone can learn from. I think Black women have a special ability to bring all kinds of people together and I hope that when people see this cover, they feel that, plus see that I had a lot of fun creating it all the while.

Dear reader,

Thank you for picking up this book and welcome to the worldwide BK community! You're joining a special group of people who have come together to create positive change in their lives, organizations, and communities.

What's BK all about?

Our mission is to connect people and ideas to create a world that works for all.

Why? Our communities, organizations, and lives get bogged down by old paradigms of self-interest, exclusion, hierarchy, and privilege. But we believe that can change. That's why we seek the leading experts on these challenges—and share their actionable ideas with you.

A welcome gift

To help you get started, we'd like to offer you a **free copy** of one of our bestselling ebooks:

www.bkconnection.com/welcome

When you claim your **free ebook**, you'll also be subscribed to our blog.

Our freshest insights

Access the best new tools and ideas for leaders at all levels on our blog at ideas.bkconnection.com.

Sincerely,

Your friends at Berrett-Koehler

Certified

Corporation